Cambridge Elements ≡

Elements in International Relations
edited by
Jon C. W. Pevehouse
University of Wisconsin-Madison
Tanja A. Börzel
Freie Universität Berlin
Edward D. Mansfield
University of Pennsylvania

ACROSS TYPE, TIME AND SPACE

*American Grand Strategy in
Comparative Perspective*

Peter Dombrowski
Naval War College

Simon Reich
*Rutgers, Newark and Le Centre de recherches
internationals, Sciences Po (Paris)*

CAMBRIDGE
UNIVERSITY PRESS

University Printing House, Cambridge CB2 8BS, United Kingdom

One Liberty Plaza, 20th Floor, New York, NY 10006, USA

477 Williamstown Road, Port Melbourne, VIC 3207, Australia

314–321, 3rd Floor, Plot 3, Splendor Forum, Jasola District Centre, New Delhi – 110025, India

79 Anson Road, #06–04/06, Singapore 079906

Cambridge University Press is part of the University of Cambridge.

It furthers the University's mission by disseminating knowledge in the pursuit of education, learning, and research at the highest international levels of excellence.

www.cambridge.org
Information on this title: www.cambridge.org/9781108972901
DOI: 10.1017/9781108973274

First published in 2021

A catalogue record for this publication is available from the British Library.

ISBN 978-1-108-97290-1 Paperback
ISSN 2515-706X (online)
ISSN 2515-7302 (print)

Across Type, Time and Space

American Grand Strategy in Comparative Perspective

Elements in International Relations

DOI: 10.1017/9781108973274
First published online: May 2021

Peter Dombrowski
Naval War College

Simon Reich
Rutgers, Newark and Le Centre de recherches internationales, Sciences Po (Paris)

Author for correspondence: Peter Dombrowski, dombrowp@usnwc.edu

Abstract: The field of grand strategy is exceptionally American-centric – theoretically, methodologically and empirically. Indeed, many scholars treat the United States as a unique case, and thus incomparable. This Element addresses the shortcomings of this approach by developing a novel framework for the purpose of systematic comparison, both within and among different countries. Using the United States as a benchmark, three dimensions are considered in which grand strategy can be compared: first, attributes of the major types commonly discussed in the literature; second, similarities and differences in the implementation of grand strategies over time, using US strategic relations with contemporary Russia as an example; and finally, across space, properties of the grand strategies that are interactively employed by other major powers in relation to the United States in the Indo-Pacific. The Element can be used by scholars and students alike to expand analysis beyond the confines that currently dominate the field.

Keywords: American grand strategy, China, comparative grand strategy, deep engagement, diplomacy, economic strategy, European security, foreign policy, India, Indo-Pacific, isolationism, Liberal order, military strategy, NATO, primacy, sponsorship, restraint, Russia

ISBNs: 9781108972901 (PB), 9781108973274 (OC)
ISSNs: 2515-706X (online), 2515-7302 (print)

Contents

1. Grand Strategy: Comparing across Time, Type and Space

The academic study of grand strategy in the field of international relations (IR) overwhelmingly focuses on the United States. The great scholarly debates often emphasize prescription – which kind of grand strategy the United States ought to pursue – rather than explaining, for example, why the United States pursues a particular strategy at a particular time.[1] The preponderance of research on other countries examines great power contenders, notably China and Russia.[2] That work is generally more analytic and explanatory, although there is a propensity to ruminate about what the United States should do in response.[3] Historians contribute significantly to the study of grand strategy. Their narratives are informative, contextual and often include a comparative component such as the study of leadership, of empires or of states in particular circumstances – such as great powers preceding or during wars.[4]

Neither group, however, provides a framework to systematically compare grand strategies across different dimensions. We attempt to address these lacunae in this Element. Our goal is to offer a framework that scholars can use to compare grand strategies in three dimensions – across type, time and space. Recognizing that the United States dominates the field, we do this by using it as our initial benchmark. Hence our subtitle: *American Grand Strategy in Comparative Perspective*. But, as we move through successive sections, we shift away from a focus on the United States to develop a framework in which it is just another – albeit important – state.

In section 2 we introduce a framework built on six questions that can be applied to the notion of comparison in all three dimensions: across *types* of grand strategy, across *time* in terms of the prevalent grand strategy within any state and

---

[1] See, as examples, Stephen G. Brooks and William C. Wohlforth, *America Abroad: Why the Sole Superpower Should Not Pull Back from the World* (London: Oxford University Press, 2016); Daniel Deudney and John Ikenberry, *Democratic Internationalism: An American Grand Strategy for a Post-Exceptionalist Era* (New York: Council on Foreign Relations, November 15, 2012), www.cfr.org/report/democratic-internationalism; Barry R. Posen, *Restraint: A New Foundation for Grand Strategy* (Ithaca, NY: Cornell University Press, 2014); Stephen M. Walt, *Taming American Power: The Global Response to U.S. Primacy* (New York: Norton, 2005).

[2] On China, see Avery Goldstein, *Rising to the Challenge – China's Grand Strategy and International Security* (Stanford, CA: Stanford University Press, 2005); Michael D. Swaine and Ashley J. Tellis, *Interpreting China's Grand Strategy: Past, Present and Future* (Santa Monic, CA: Rand Corporation, 2000); Sulmaan Wasif Khan, *Haunted by Chaos: China's Grand Strategy from Mao Zedong to Xi Jinping* (Cambridge, MA: Harvard University Press, 2018). On Russia, see Andrew Monaghan, "Putin's Russia: 'Shaping a Grand Strategy',." *International Affairs* 89, no. 5 (September, 2013): pp. 1221–1236.

[3] Michael McFaul, "The Grand Strategy of Vladimir Putin," *Hoover Digest*, no. 1 (January 30, 2004), www.hoover.org/publications/hoover-digest/article/7634.

[4] See, as examples, John Lewis Gaddis, *On Grand Strategy* (New York: Penguin Press, 2018); Paul Kennedy, ed. *Grand Strategy in War and Peace* (New Haven, CT: Yale University Press, 1991); Edward N. Luttwak, *The Grand Strategy of the Byzantine Empire* (Cambridge, MA: Harvard University Press, 2009).

subsequently across *space*, meaning an examination (and possibly comparison) of individual state strategies, potentially whether those are great, regional or smaller powers.

These questions attempt to reveal both the similarities and the differences between different national grand strategies, as well as their sources of continuity and change in a dynamic global environment. While not exhaustive, they extend from rudimentary questions about the working definition and scope of a grand strategy to its underlying assumptions, its conception (in the customary language of the literature) of a grand strategy's "ends," "ways" and "means," and, crucially, its characterization of – and balance between – threats and opportunities. Surprisingly, these elements have not yet been rigorously compared to generate an analytic framework. Definitions and assumptions are contested, but there are few explicitly causal theories about grand strategies themselves, and we argue that comparison is a central part of that process.[5]

We then apply threads of this framework in the three dimensions in successive sections. Section 3 examines the types of grand strategies that states may potentially pursue, our analysis extending beyond most current typologies that confine the definition of grand strategies to a narrow national security orientation. It includes alternatives that address anthropogenic and naturogenic threats such as climate change and pandemics. This section is, admittedly, heavily focused on the United States and we acknowledge that many of the options may not apply to other states. Nonetheless, as we will discuss, even regional or smaller powers may adopt aspects of these strategies under specific circumstances.

Existing typologies present problems. The substance of grand strategies is often assumed to be limited to armed conflict. The overuse of shorthand labels obscures important nuances. Unilateralism and coercion, for example, are associated with realist forms of primacy and the label is shortened even further by references to the world's "goliath," "sheriff" or "policeman."[6] Multilateralism, international order and institution building are associated with notions of cooperative security, liberal hegemony and grandiose American conceptions of itself as an "indispensable power."[7] The result is often counterproductive for both scholarly and public debate

---

[5] Paul C. Avey, Jonathan N. Markowitz and Robert J. Reardon, "Disentangling Grand Strategy: International Relations Theory and U.S. Grand Strategy," *Texas National Security Review* 2, no. 1 (November, 2018), http://dx.doi.org/10.26153/tsw/869.

[6] Richard N. Haass, *The Reluctant Sheriff: The United States after the Cold War* (New York: Council on Foreign Relations Press, 1997); Michael Mandelbaum, *The Case for Goliath: How America Acts As the World's Government in the Twenty-First Century* (New York: Public Affairs, 2005); Joshua Muravchik, *The Imperative of American Leadership* (Washington, DC: American Enterprise Institute, 1996).

[7] The term was first associated with Madeleine K. Albright in an interview on NBC-TV's "The Today Show" with Matt Lauer (Columbus, Ohio, February 19, 1998). But President Obama reiterated American indispensability in, for example, "President Obama: What

where, for example, "Ending Never-ending Wars" has become shorthand for a grand strategy of restraint,[8] obfuscating questions about the forms and degree of any offshore military deployment.

Succinct labels are understandable in public debates where deliberative assessments are often sacrificed to soundbites. But they are less acceptable in scholarly debates because they obscure rather than add nuance and analytic insight. Nuance can help establish causal relationships and support strategic decision-making.[9] Consider this statement by Patrick Porter:

> Long before the fall of the Soviet Union, the United States formed a grand strategy of "primacy," often coined as "leadership." This strategy was interrupted only occasionally. By the 1960s, it had set the parameters for Washington's foreign policy debate. The strategy has four interlocking parts: to be militarily preponderant; to reassure and contain allies; to integrate other states into U.S.-designed institutions and markets; and to inhibit the spread of nuclear weapons.[10]

Here, Porter conflates two significantly different approaches: primacy and "deep engagement." Two components of Porter's "four interlocking parts" are primarily associated with primacy (military preponderance and inhibiting the spread of nuclear weapons). But the other pair (with their focus on allies and institution building) are more associated with deep engagement.[11]

Collapsing them into one is problematic because their underlying assumptions – and ways, means and ends – vastly differ, with significant theoretical and policy implications. In general, a primacist grand strategy is expensive (in terms of the "means" used) and relies preponderantly on overwhelming military power.[12] In contrast, deep engagement incurs, but also shares, material burdens and requires a greater range of policy instruments (from alliance diplomacy to

Makes Us America," September 28, 2014, www.cbsnews.com/news/president-obama-60-minutes/. For examples that invoke this idea see Daniel Deudney and G. JohnIkenberry, *Democratic Internationalism: An American Grand Strategy for a Post-Exceptionalist Era* (New York: Council on Foreign Relations, 2012), p. 1.

[8] See "About QI," Quincy Institute for Responsible Statecraft (undated), https://quincyinst.org/about/.

[9] Academics are often characterized as having little influence on policymakers. Yet, under Trump, while James Mattis served as Secretary of Defense, he was reputed to have read the work of, and met with, notable scholars working in the field of American grand strategy. On causation in studies of grand strategy see Thierry Balzacq, Peter Dombrowski and Simon Reich, "Is Grand Strategy a Research Program? A Review Essay," *Security Studies* 28, no. 1 (2019): pp. 58–86, https://doi.org/10.1080/09636412.2018.1508631.

[10] Patrick Porter, "Why America's Grand Strategy Has Not Changed: Power, Habit, and the U.S. Foreign Policy Establishment," *International Security* 42, no. 4 (Spring, 2018): p. 9.

[11] Ibid.

[12] On the costs, particularly how much primacy contributes to the federal deficit, see Carla Norrlof and William Wohlforth, "Is US Grand Strategy Self-Defeating? Deep Engagement, Military Spending, and Sovereign Debt," *Conflict Management and Peace Science* 36, no. 3 (2019): pp.

aid, economic multilateralism and global and regional institution-building). These differences become starker when other grand strategies – such as sponsorship, restraint or isolationism – are factored in.

We then extend the analysis to comparison over time in section 4. Historians have wrestled with this issue. Hal Brands, for example, compares the relationship between presidents and the US Congress in the second half of the twentieth century.[13] John Gaddis has offered a series of comparative enduring "principles" that scholars should bear in mind.[14] But few approximate the requisites of Alexander George's structured-focused comparison or process tracing (what George called "the historian's methodology") to systematically compare a state's strategy over time.[15]

Utilizing the same set of questions, we compare the continuities and changes in American grand strategy over the course of the first three American presidencies of the twenty-first century – those of George W. Bush, Barack Obama and Donald Trump. Our goal is to examine where they converged and contrasted. To do so effectively, we focus our attention on Europe because of its vital, long-standing strategic importance. President Trump's periodic hostile diatribes and confrontational policies concerning military (notably NATO), economic (regarding trade practices), and public health (the Coronavirus travel ban) issues signaled a growing impatience with America's traditional European allies. Nonetheless, we identify notable elements of both continuity and change across the three administrations.

In section 5, we expand across space to compare US grand strategy to that of two other states: China, already a great power competitor, and India, an emergent power with aspirations to become a great power. We examine two dimensions. The first is how each state has constructed a guiding architecture for their grand strategy.[16] The second concerns how each state, dynamically and interactively, responds to the other's grand strategy as they balance between shaping and adapting to emergent threats and opportunities.

Space limitations dictate that our empirical presentation can only be illustrative. We focus on an emergent, dynamic region – the vast expanse of

---

227–247. On the benefits, see Daniel W. Drezner, "Military Primacy Doesn't Pay (Nearly As Much As You Think)," *International Security* 38, no. 1 (Summer, 2013): pp. 52–79.

[13] Hal Brands, *What Good Is Grand Strategy? Power and Purpose in American Statecraft from Harry S. Truman to George W. Bush* (Ithaca, NY: Cornell University Press, 2015).

[14] Gaddis, *On Grand Strategy*.

[15] Alexander George, "Case Study and Theory Development: The Method of Structured, Focused Comparison" in *Diplomacy: New Approaches in History, Theory and Policy*, ed. Paul Gordon (New York: Free Press, 1979), pp. 43–68; Christine Trampusch and Bruno Palier, "Between X and Y: How Process Tracing Contributes to Opening the Black Box of Causality," *New Political Economy* 21, no. 5 (2016): pp. 437–454.

[16] Brands, *What Good Is Grand Strategy?* p. 3.

the redefined Indo-Pacific, which successive administrations have characterized as the strategically most important region with regard to American interests in the twenty-first century. Here, however, American grand strategy becomes more of a context against which we examine those of the other two states – China and India – deliberately chosen because they reflect a variety of goals, instruments and resources. This comparison, albeit limited in scope, generates an interesting finding: Contrary to conventional assumptions about American grand strategy being determinative, China has in fact been the primary shaper of the region's dynamics, with India and the United States adapting in response.

In a brief conclusion (section 6) we turn to two overriding questions: how to think about a comparative research program in the field of grand strategy that does not begin with the United States as the dominant case, and what kinds of questions might both academics and policymakers focus on if they decide that a program in comparative grand strategy has its virtues.

2. Contrasting Assumptions and a Comparative Framework

The field of grand strategy is replete with problems that undermine its capacity to evolve into a conventional research program.[17] Definitions are contested and thus the choice of what to actually study is unresolved: Work is often prescriptive, rather than focusing on explanation;[18] there are few notable explicitly causal theories about grand strategy itself;[19] and the question of how to compare hasn't reasonably been debated, let alone settled.[20]

The focus of a research program should be on generating a series of generalizable formulations extending well beyond a very limited universe of cases. According to George Alexander and Richard Smoke, it should

---

[17] See Imre Lakatos, "Falsification and the Methodology of Scientific Research Programmes" in *Criticism and the Growth of Knowledge*, ed. Imre Lakatos and Alan Musgrave (Cambridge, UK: Cambridge University Press, 1970), pp. 122–131. For a more digestible formulation of Lakatos's argument that addresses issues central to the field of international relations, see Rudra Sil and Peter Katzenstein, *Beyond Paradigms: Analytic Eclecticism in the Study of World Politics* (London: Palgrave Macmillan, 2010), particularly pp. 5–13.

[18] Barry Posen reflected the tendency toward prescription when expressing a common sentiment that "The [realist] theories that inform my strategic thinking, and the particular facts of the U.S. situation, suggest that US grand strategy can and should be quite 'restrained' " (Posen, *Restraint*, p. 23). Yet he does not explicitly discuss those theories and how they relate to his prescription. He uses an implicit causal logic rather than explicit theory as the basis for prescription.

[19] For an affirmation of the latter see Avey, Markowitz and Reardon, "Disentangling Grand Strategy."

[20] For a specific application to the field of grand strategy, see Balzacq, Dombrowski and Reich, "Is Grand Strategy a Research Program?"

concentrate on diagnostics, not prescription.[21] Among the challenges facing scholars are answers to questions such as why states adopt and then change their grand strategies; if, when and how these change the nature of the international system itself; and what determines how domestic national security institutions actually implement strategic visions.

We cannot address all these issues in the context of this short Element. But developing a comparative framework has utility for addressing aspects of them in a way that may encourage further debate. Answering questions like what drives a particular type of grand strategy would engender a rich field of inquiry. This work may guide us toward eventual diagnosis, rather than prescription.

In this section, we briefly offer a set of assumptions that we believe are foundational for future comparative research on grand strategy, a requisite if the field is to offer generalizable and testable theoretical propositions. We then outline a framework for future comparative work on grand strategy.

2.1 The Contrasting Assumptions of Comparative Grand Strategy

In constructing a case for comparative grand strategy, we begin by disputing the common view that all policymakers are exclusively rational in their calculations when making decisions, as well as how they calculate and what they calculate about. We assume, rather, that grand strategizing has subjective, cognitive, and cultural elements.[22] Decision-making by state elites about goals, threats, opportunities and the means of implementing a grand strategy are conditioned by a confluence of subjective and objective factors. Restated paradigmatically, Realists and Liberals have dominated the debate, Constructivists have played

---

[21] Alexander George and Richard Smoke, *Deterrence in American Foreign Policy: Theory and Practice* (New York: Columbia University Press, 1974), p. 636. Work that emphasizes prescription is too voluminous to cite comprehensively here, but for recent important examples, see Rebecca Friedman Lissner and Mira Rapp- Hooper, "The Day after Trump: American Strategy for a New International Order," *Washington Quarterly* 41 (2018): pp. 7–25; John J. Mearsheimer and Stephen M. Walt, "The Case for Offshore Balancing," *Foreign Affairs* 95 (July–August, 2016): pp. 70–83; Ionut Popscu, "American Grand Strategy and the Rise of Offensive Realism," *Political Science Quarterly* 134, no. 3 (2018-19): pp. 375–405; Barry R. Posen, "Pull Back: The Case for a Less Activist Foreign Policy," *Foreign Affairs* 92 (January–February, 2013): pp. 105–116; Stephen M. Walt, *The Hell of Good Intentions: America's Foreign Policy Elite and the Decline of U.S. Primacy* (New York: Farrar, Straus and Giroux, 2018).

[22] For examples from other parts of the IR literature on cognitive and cultural processes of decision-making, see Richard Ned Lebow, *Nuclear Crisis Management* (Ithaca, NY: Cornell University Press, 1985); Robert Jervis, Richard Ned Lebow and Janice Gross Stein, *Psychology and Deterrence* (Baltimore, MD: The Johns Hopkins University Press, 1984,); Robert Jervis, "Cooperation under the Security Dilemma," *World Politics* 30, no. 2 (January, 1978): pp. 167–214; Peter J. Katzenstein, *The Culture of National Security: Norms and Identity in World Politics* (New York: Columbia University Press, 1996); and Alastair Iain Johnston, "Thinking About Strategic Culture," *International Security* 19, no. 4 (Spring, 1995): pp. 32–64.

a marginal role, and Marxists have abstained although they offer trenchant criticism.[23]

How state elites interpret, and reinterpret, history helps define goals, prioritize threats and opportunities and marshal resources. A collective sense of historical injustice and victimhood, of the need to resurrect lost empire or even guilt, is adjudicated through domestic politics and sold to waiting publics. Such factors often prove as important as the pressures of the external environment in interpreting threats. Albanians and Kosovars still focus on the Serbian threat despite the passage of a generation since the end of the Balkan wars.[24] Turkey's leaders seek to rekindle the Ottoman Empire lost a century ago.[25] In several countries (such as Iran or Saudi Arabia) confessional politics and religious aspirations underpin strategic choices, a circumstance long unimaginable in most Western countries.[26]

Second, we therefore assume that domestic politics plays a far greater explanatory role in the formulation and implementation of a grand strategy. As we discuss in greater detail in section 3, some Realists acknowledge the effect of domestic economic capacity on a military budget, but little more.[27] Liberal proponents of deep engagement *plus* promote values such as democracy. Neoclassical Realists contend that the relationship between systemic and

---

[23] For Constructivist exceptions, see Stacie E. Goddard and Ronald R. Krebs, "Rhetoric, Legitimation, and Grand Strategy," *Security Studies* 24, no. 1 (2015): pp. 5–36; Ian Clark, *Legitimacy in International Society* (New York: Oxford University Press, 2007); Ronald R. Krebs, *Narrative and the Making of US National Security* (Cambridge, UK:Cambridge University Press, 2015). For an assessment of the role of strategic culture, see Alastair Iain Johnston, *Cultural Realism: Strategic Culture and Grand Strategy in Chinese History* (Princeton, NJ: Princeton University Press, 1998); Jeffrey S. Lantis, 'Strategic Culture: From Clausewitz to Constructivism" in *Strategic Culture and Weapons of Mass Destruction: Culturally Based Insights into Comparative National Security Policymaking*, ed. Jeannie L. Johnson, Kerry M. Kartchner and Jeffrey A. Larsen (New York: Palgrave MacMillan, 2009). On Marxism, see Perry Anderson, *American Foreign Policy and Its Thinkers* (New York: Verso, 2015), especially p. 155.

[24] "Freedom and Fear: Kosovo Remembers War, 20 Years After," *RFI*, November 6, 2019, www.rfi.fr/en/contenu/20190611-freedom-and-fear-kosovo-remembers-war-20-years-after.

[25] Michael Colborne and Maxim Edwards, "Erdogan Is Making the Ottoman Empire Great Again," *Foreign Policy*, June 22, 2018, https://foreignpolicy.com/2018/06/22/erdogan-is-making-the-ottoman-empire-great-again/.

[26] Michael Axworthy, *Iran (What Everyone Needs to Know)* (London: Oxford University Press, 2017), pp. 173–180; Crystal A. Ennis and Bessma Momani, "Shaping the Middle East in the Midst of the Arab Uprisings: Turkish and Saudi Foreign Policy Strategies," *Third World Quarterly* 34, no. 6 (2013): pp. 1127–1144.

[27] The debated is linked in at least two ways: first, whether maintaining primacy is worth it (see, for example, Drezner, "Military Primacy Doesn't Pay") and second, whether the case for restraint based on the negative impacts on the US economy, such as increasing the nation's debt, is true: "[An] oft-expressed economic argument against the United States globally engaged grand strategy – that the military expenditures it entails is responsible for escalating debt – lacks grounding in empirical evidence and economic theory" (Norrlof and Wohlforth, "Is US Grand Strategy Self-Defeating?," p. 243).

domestic factors is interactive,[28] but leave unresolved the question of causality in that relationship, arguing "that employing such an approach makes it difficult to say much about the causal role of power factors relative to other potential independent variables."[29]

We regard domestic factors as causative in defining the ways, means and ends of grand strategy. This assumption helps us interrogate how institutional factors influence the resilience of grand strategy in some countries, long after the geopolitical circumstances have demanded strategic adjustment.[30] Famously, France tried to maintain its colonialist power in Algeria and Indo–China long after domestic and international circumstances suggested that withdrawal would have been less costly.[31] The same was true of Britain, which failed to recognize that even victory in World War II would necessitate the decline of the role of the pound Sterling and the end of empire.[32]

Third, we assume that any coherent state can potentially develop a grand strategy utilizing different configurations of diplomatic, economic and/or military instruments.[33] Even some supra-state or nonstate actors – such as the EU, Taliban or ISIS – do so as well.[34] We do, however, exclude failed or fragile states – such as Libya, Somalia or Yemen – as possibilities. They lack the capacity to formulate and implement a grand strategy. We also reject states that are demonstrably not autonomous from their neighbors, such as Belarus which is reliant on Russia.

---

[28] Jeffrey W. Taliaferro, Norrin M. Ripsman and Steven E. Lobell, eds., *The Challenge of Grand Strategy: The Great Powers and the Broken Balance between the Wars* (Cambridge, UK: Cambridge University Press, 2012).

[29] Gideon Rose, "Neoclassical Realism and Theories of Foreign Policy," *World Politics* 51, no. 1 (October, 1998): p. 151. See also, Valerie M. Hudson, "Foreign Policy Analysis: Actor-Specific Theory and the Ground of International Relations," *Foreign Policy Analysis* 1, no. 1 (March, 2005): pp. 1–30.

[30] On domestic factors and strategic adjustment, see Peter Trubowitz, Emily Goldman and Edward Rhodes, eds., *The Politics of Strategic Adjustment: Ideas, Interests and Institutions* (New York: Columbia University Press, 1998).

[31] Raymond Aron, *La tragedie Algerienne* (Paris: Plon, 1957).

[32] Peter Clarke, *The Last Thousand Days of the British Empire* (New York: Bloomsbury Press, 2008).

[33] Goddard and Krebs, "Rhetoric, Legitimation, and Grand Strategy."

[34] On the EU, see Jolyon Howorth, "The EU As a Global Actor: Grand Strategy for a Global Grand Bargain," *Journal of Common Market Studies* 48, no. 3 (June, 2010): pp. 455–474; Daniel Fiott and Luis Simón, "The European Union," in *Comparative Grand Strategy: A Framework and Case*, eds. Thierry Balzacq, Peter Dombrowski and Simon Reich (New York: Oxford University Press, 2019), pp. 263–283. For the case of the Taliban, for example, see Mohammed Kakar, *Afghanistan: The Soviet Invasion and the Afghan Response, 1979–1982* (Berkeley, CA: University of California Press, 1995); and Seth G. Jones, *In the Graveyard of Empires: America's War in Afghanistan* (New York: Norton, 2010). On ISIS see Ahmed S. Hashim, "The Islamic State: From Al-Qaeda Affiliate to Caliphate," *Middle East Policy* 21 no. 4 (Winter, 2014): pp. 69–83.

Where a decision has to be made about whether a state qualifies for study, however, the burden should be on scholars to explore the details of whether and how a state can engineer its own security, rather than simply assuming it cannot. We begin by asking a question: Does a particular state demonstrate the requisite capacity to formulate grand strategic goals, an ability to make independent decisions and the means to implement them, even if this architecture does not resemble Western idealized notions of policy making? The utility of this approach is threefold: increasing the prospects of generalizability; a comparative capacity for establishing causality; and a greater ability for policymakers to recognize the interactive nature of any grand strategy.

Fourth, grand strategies do not have to focus exclusively on controlling or shaping the global system – that is, trying to impose their own worldview on their external environment.[35] They can also adapt to the exigencies of that system, or detach from it through an autarkic approach. All states with a grand strategy – great or small – attempt to combine both elements of controlling or shaping, and adaption or detachment – locally, regionally or globally – to varying degrees. The variation among the grand strategies of individual states is their capacity to balance these elements. The United States, for example, may seek to control or shape but, in practice, it also routinely adapts to systemic changes such as responding to the rise of what it characterizes as "revisionist powers" like China in the Indo–Pacific and Russia in the Arctic, Baltics and beyond.[36]

Smaller states, by necessity, often emphasize adaptation or detachment in their grand strategies. Critics of this assumption characterize this behavior as merely "strategic." But, in practice, the distinction between grand strategy and strategy is often blurred.[37] It would be hard to classify North Korea's behavior over seven decades as only "strategic" or tactical. It has shaped the northeast Asian region while remaining largely detached. Both Israeli strategies and

---

[35] On the difference between shaping and controlling, see Barry R. Posen, "Command of the Commons: The Military Foundation of U.S. Hegemony," *International Security* 28, no. 1 (Summer, 2003): pp. 5–46.

[36] See Anne Applebaum, "Putin's Grand Strategy," *South Central Review* 35, no. 1 (Spring, 2018): pp. 22–34, https://muse.jhu.edu/article/690689/pdf; Monaghan, "Putin's Russia"; McFaul, "The Grand Strategy of Vladimir Putin"; Robert Person, "Russian Grand Strategy in the 21st Century," *NSI*, May 3, 2019, https://nsiteam.com/russian-grand-strategy-in-the-21st-century/.

[37] For varied perspectives on this issue, see David A. Baldwin, "The Concept of Security," *Review of International Studies* 23, no. 1 (January, 1997): pp. 5–26; Richard K. Betts "Should Strategic Studies Survive?," *World Politics* 50, no. 1 (October, 1997): pp. 7–33; Colin S. Gray, "Approaching the Study of Strategy" in *International Security and War: Politics and Grand Strategy in the 21st Century*, ed. Ralph Rotte and Christoph Schwartz (New York: Nova, 2011); Lukas Milevski, *The Evolution of Modern Grand Strategic Thought* (London: Oxford University Press, 2016); Stephen M. Walt, "The Renaissance of Security Studies," *International Studies Quarterly* 31, no. 2 (June,1991): pp. 211–239.

tactics over the last decade and Iranian strategy since 1979 have at times shaped the Middle Eastern political, diplomatic and security environment.[38] None of these efforts seek to control the global environment like, for example, China's Belt and Road Initiative (see section 5). Nor are they comparable in terms of geographic scope. But their significance for the security environments in which they operate – locally and regionally in terms of their neighbors – should not be underestimated. Each region's security environment would alter considerably if there were regimes with different grand strategies in Iran, North Korea and Israel.

Our fifth assumption is that states can and do employ numerous instruments (means) to address a growing variety of perceived threats and opportunities (ends). Kinetic conflict and liberal-democratic values are still too limited in defining the boundaries of the ends of grand strategy, as are the instruments employed, in an evolving global environment. In our 2018 book *The End of Grand Strategy* we laid out an argument for a threefold typology of threats that grand strategy can and does seek to address: kinetic, anthropogenic (such as climate change) and naturogenic (such as viruses) threats. Combatting them uses far more instruments than the grand strategy literature acknowledges.[39] The World Health Organization's 2019 estimate of a quarter of a million deaths a year from the effects of climate change, for example, is clearly a conservative number.[40] Likewise, the US rhetoric regarding COVID-19 (describing it as a "war"), the transnational process of transmission, the invocation of National Defense legislation, the adoption of emergency measures including the use of the military, and the mortality rate (higher than the Korean and Vietnam wars combined), all legitimate the idea that combatting epidemics should be a goal of grand strategy, comparable to fighting a war.[41] Accepting that assumption, and with it a redefinition of national security, also expands the possible instruments that can be used in any grand strategy (the "means–ends" linkage).[42] The instruments of public health are analytically commensurate with the instruments of war. The ends–means linkage may extend much further. Generating

[38] See Eitan Shamir, "Israel," and Thierry Balzacq and Wendy Ramadan-Alban "Iran," both in Balzacq, Dombrowski and Reich *Comparative Grand Strategy*.

[39] Simon Reich and Peter Dombrowski, *The End of Grand Strategy* (Ithaca, NY: Cornell University Press, 2018), pp. 20–22.

[40] Jen Christensen, "250,000 Deaths a Year from Climate Change is a 'Conservative Estimate,' Research Says," *CNN*, January 16, 2019, www.cnn.com/2019/01/16/health/climate-change-health-emergency-study/index.html.

[41] Charlie Savage, "How the Defense Production Act Could Yield More Masks, Ventilators and Tests," *New York Times*, March 20, 2020, www.nytimes.com/2020/03/20/us/politics/defense-production-act-virus.html.

[42] Anne-Marie Slaughter, "Redefining National Security for the Post-Pandemic World," *Project Syndicate*, June 3, 2020, www.project-syndicate.org/commentary/redefining-national-security-for-world-after-covid19-by-anne-marie-slaughter-2020-06.

and exporting solar power to Europe, for example, has become a, if not the, central plank of Morocco's development policy in the context of climate change.[43] China has used the opportunity afforded by the Coronavirus to demonstrate its generosity in providing materials and otherwise cooperating with other states as part of a broader strategic charm offensive.[44]

Collectively, these five assumptions expand the aperture for analyzing grand strategy in a much larger universe of cases. Failing to acknowledge the fact that so many countries use so many tools to achieve so many legitimate goals is symptomatic of both an intellectual gap among some scholars of grand strategy and a policy flaw that may affect the ability of the United States to achieve its strategic objectives in an increasingly competitive international environment.

2.2 A Framework for Analysis

We now provide a framework for comparison that we believe has utility in all three dimensions: across types of grand strategies, across time (looking at different national administrations or governments) and – ultimately – across different states. The framework is predicated on questions essential to understanding any national grand strategy.

2.2.1 What Is the Definition and Scope?

Lukas Milevski points out that there is no agreed definition of grand strategy.[45] Scholarship is essentially divided between the *classical* and *IR* definitions, each generating a differing logic and scope.[46]

The classical approach assumes that the primary purpose of grand strategy is to prepare for and to win wars. Contemporary Realists adopt a variant of this approach. Barry Posen suggests that:

> Grand strategy focuses on military threats, because these are the most dangerous, and military remedies because these are the most costly. Security has traditionally encompassed the preservation of sovereignty, safety, territorial integrity, and power position – the last being the necessary means to the first

---

[43] Salman Zafar, "Renewable Energy in Morocco," *EcoMena*, December 22, 2017, www.ecomena.org/renewable-energy-in-morocco/.

[44] See, as examples, "Mask Diplomacy: China tries to Rewrite Coronavirus Narrative," *Straits Times*, March 20, 2020, www.straitstimes.com/asia/east-asia/mask-diplomacy-china-tries-to-rewrite-coronavirus-narrative; Lynn Kuok, "Will COVID-19 Change the Geopolitics of the Indo-Pacific?," *IISS*, June 4, 2020, www.iiss.org/blogs/analysis/2020/06/geopolitics-covid-19-indo-pacific?fbclid=IwAR1JBeYxjdZsKm5pyTo_b-tYedTFDhP8jTl50uqeYexQOq84z6anRh5DldQ.

[45] Lukas Milevski, *The Evolution of Modern Grand Strategic Thought* (Oxford: Oxford University Press, 2016), pp. 1, 25, 104, 127.

[46] Balzacq, Dombrowski and Reich, "Is Grand Strategy a Research Program?"

three … A grand strategy contains explanations for why threats enjoy a certain priority, and why and how the remedies proposed could work.[47]

A grand strategy's core scope is to address "direct, imminent, and plausible military threats by other nation-states."[48] For Colin Gray, grand strategy, strategy, and national security policy are aligned (and potentially indistinguishable).[49] Robert Art likewise suggests that scholars who focus exclusively on kinetic threats concentrate primarily on state interests and how "the military instrument should be employed to realize them."[50]

IR oriented scholars do not coalesce around a single purpose. But some take their cues from B. H. Liddell Hart who contended that grand strategy was about winning wars and periods of peace.[51] This view presaged a "hearts and minds" strategy that belatedly became emblematic of the American postwar reconstruction approach.[52] Paul Kennedy encapsulates this view when suggesting that "The crux of grand strategy … lies … in the capacity of the nation's leaders to bring together all the elements, both military and non-military, for the preservation and enhancement of the nation's long-term (that is, in wartime and in peacetime) best interests."[53]

Grand strategy, William Martel argues, "is not and never has been simply about war or the conduct of war – in fact, war often represents a failure of grand strategy."[54] Rather, its scope may include building credibility abroad as a way of engaging allies and constraining adversaries across a variety of domains. This logic applies to both Liberals who focus on American leadership and institution building and Constructivists focusing on legitimacy and norm building.[55] Liberals have expanded the scope of grand strategy to incorporate elements of the rule of law, as well as the spread of liberal capitalism, democracy, human rights and even humanitarian intervention as a tool in a version labeled "deep engagement plus."[56] Others, advocating a sponsorship strategy, have emphasized the significance of global organizations and protocols in justifying action to address collective action

---

[47] Posen, *Restraint*, p. 1.
[48] Ibid., p. 3.
[49] Gray, "Approaching the Study of Strategy."
[50] Robert J. Art, *A Grand Strategy for America* (Ithaca, NY: Cornell University Press, 2004), p. 10.
[51] Basil Henry Liddell Hart, *Strategy* (London: Faber & Faber, 1967, 2nd rev. ed.), p.322.
[52] Jason C. Parker, *Hearts, Minds, Voices: US Cold War Public Diplomacy and the Formation of the Third World* (New York: Oxford University Press, 2016).
[53] Paul Kennedy, "Grand Strategy in War and Peace: Toward a Broader Definition" in *Grand Strategy in War and Peace*, ed. Paul Kennedy (New Haven, CT: Yale University Press, 1991), p. 5.
[54] William C. Martel, *Grand Strategy in Theory and Practice: The Need for an Effective American Foreign Policy* (New York: Cambridge University Press, 2015), p. 4; on legitimacy see pp. 97 and 101.
[55] G. John Ikenberry, *Liberal Leviathan: The Origins, Crisis, and Transformation of the American World Order* (Princeton, NJ: Princeton University Press, 2011); Krebs, *Narrative and the Making of US National Security*.
[56] Brooks and Wohlforth, *America Abroad*, p. 73.

problems such as piracy, human trafficking or climate change.[57] The first question therefore concerns which working definition a state employs and, correspondingly, how expansive the scope of that definition is in practice.

2.2.2 What Are the Underlying Assumptions of a Grand Strategy?

Foundational assumptions generally remain implicit in the literature on grand strategy.[58] But they are often relevant because different formulations employ some overlapping assumptions yet generate different strategies and subsequent policy prescriptions.

In this section we identify five key assumptions that should ideally be explicitly addressed by any typology of grand strategy. First, the central actors – who they are, how heterogeneous they are and what roles they play. Different approaches to grand strategy range from state-centric assumptions to those that emphasize the significance of legitimate (corporations or foundations) or illegitimate (terrorists, militias or transnational criminals) actors.[59] Second, is the question of the assumed relationship between actors in a grand strategy: whether they are conflictual, competitive or collaborative. This distinction conditions a third assumption, about the operating principles of a grand strategy, which run along a spectrum spanning from hierarchical domination or benign hegemony to adjuvant guidance, deference, submission or degrees of strategic detachment. These operating principles link to a fourth assumption about the degrees and forms of strategic coordination with other actors. This spans from unilateral or bilateral to multilaterally coordinated rule – or norm-driven action – in the implementation of a grand strategy. Ultimately, there is a fifth assumption, the modality – or habitual responses – of a grand strategy: the principle regarding how it should operate, varying from assertive military intervention to institution building, support for international law and norms, a more limited militarized focus on "command and control" and finally deliberate inaction.

---

[57] Simon Reich and Richard Ned Lebow, *Good-bye Hegemony! Power and Influence in the Global System* (Princeton, NJ: Princeton University Press, 2014).

[58] Historians are generally more obtuse about underlying theoretical assumptions; but that is not true of all historians. John Gaddis is closely associated with realism; see for example, John Gaddis, *Strategies of Containment: A Critical Appraisal of American National Security Policy during the Cold War* (New York: Oxford University Press, 1982). And Paul Kennedy has a number of implicit realist assumptions in common with Robert Gilpin's earlier more theoretical political science work; see Paul Kennedy, *The Rise and Fall of Great Powers: Economic Change and Military Conflict from 1500 to 2000* (New York: Random House, 1987); Robert Gilpin, *War and Change in World Politics* (New York, Cambridge University Press, 1981).

[59] Office of the President, *National Security Strategy 2015* (Washington, DC: Government Publishing Office, February, 2015), https://obamawhitehouse.archives.gov/sites/default/files/docs/2015_national_security_strategy_2.pdf; Office of the President, *National Security Strategy of the United States* (Washington, DC: Government Publishing Office, December, 2017), www.whitehouse.gov/wp-content/uploads/2017/12/NSS-Final-12-18-2017-0905.pdf.

Different types of grand strategies, different national administrations and different states cluster these five assumptions in varied ways, producing a unique configuration and a basis for comparison.

2.2.3 What Are the Geostrategic Objectives (the "Ends")?

Post–Cold War American debates about objectives have habitually vied between the stabilization of the existing security order under US dominance and the consolidation of a Liberal security order in which the United States leads rather than dominates. A third, variants of retrenchment, have now been added to that debate.[60]

This American-centric approach may be analogous with other great powers but it is irrelevant to most states. A more productive way to consider the objectives of a state's grand strategy may lie among several options: Does the state primarily seek to sustain or create an advantage, redress a historical injustice (and is thus redistributive or revanchist in intent), resurrect its former powerful status (regionally or globally), restore itself as a "normal" state or, conversely, depict itself as a model for other states?[61] Each possible option is reflective of a history, tradition and culture, thus bending toward specific, different grand strategic options. While not mutually exclusive, recognizing these differing primary goals allows for comparison in terms of both differences and similarities, in ways generally not captured by the current literature.

2.2.4 What Are "the Ways"?

Ways are often difficult to conceptualize. They are conventionally depicted as planning processes according to Colonel Arthur F. Lykke's classical model, widely used in military education by the US Army despite trenchant criticism even among military educators and government officials.[62] Ways, however, can alternatively be characterized as instruments. Here, classicists focus narrowly on military tools while other professionals, including some from the military, apply broader elements of national power – diplomatic, information, military,

---

[60] For a succinct representation of all these variants and notation of the relevant literature, see Reich and Dombrowski, *The End of Grand Strategy*, pp. 32–41.

[61] Zheng Wang, *Memory Politics, Identity and Conflict: Historical Memory As a Variable* (New York: Palgrave, 2018), pp. 57–72.

[62] Arthur F. Lykke Jr., "Defining Military Strategy," *Military Review* 69, no. 5 (May, 1989): p. 3. For criticism see Linda Robinson, Paul D. Miller, John Gordon IV, Jeffrey Decker, Michael Schwille and Raphael S. Cohen, *Improving Strategic Competence: Lessons from 13 Years of War* (Arlington, VA: RAND Arroyo Center, 2014), www.rand.org/content/dam/rand/pubs/research_reports/RR800/RR816/RAND_RR816.pdf; Tami Davis Biddle, *Strategy and Grand Strategy: What Students and Practitioners Need to Know* (Carlisle, PA: Army War College Press, 2015).

economic, financial, intelligence and law enforcement (DIMEFIL).[63] Richard Kugler succinctly captures all these elements in three domains: "Political diplomacy, military power, and economic strength."[64] Militaries rely on materiel, personnel and intelligence. Beyond that, some instruments are positive in intent – states providing forms of incentives to those targeted by a grand strategy. Alliances and coalitions of the willing provide the most obvious set of positive tools along with various forms of military (such as personnel training or combat forces) and materiel (whether in the form of arms sales or aid) assistance. Great powers use these instruments routinely.

In the economic domain, positive incentives include the use of aid, preferential trade agreements, varied financial instruments and inclusion in global or regional economic institutions.[65] We associate these with great powers, but they can also be an effective tool for other states. Saudi Arabia, for example, reputedly provided $32.83 billion in aid to seventy-eight countries between 2007 and 2017, and strategically uses oil to cultivate influence.[66] Even Qatar's financial sponsorship of various countries served it well in combating a blockade imposed by other Gulf Cooperation Council states.[67]

Aid, of course, traverses both the diplomatic and military domains. Other tools in the diplomatic domain include the formal recognition (or withholding) of diplomatic status (such as the UN's and many countries' recognition of the Palestinian State) or, informally, reputational status (the Trump administration's overtures to North Korea provides a notable recent example). Informal or track-two diplomacy can also play a valuable role as an instrument, as Norway has demonstrated both multilaterally and bilaterally.[68] The balance between tools inevitably depends on the cases examined and their underlying dynamics. Track-two diplomacy may play a role in some bilateral relations and have little utility in others as our analyses in sections 4 and 5 demonstrate.

[63] United States Army Special Operations Command, "Counter-Unconventional Warfare," White Paper, September 26, 2014, p. 22, https://info.publicintelligence.net/USASOC-CounterUnconventionalWarfare.pdf.

[64] Richard L. Kugler, *Policy Analysis in National Security Affairs: New Methods for a New Era* (Washington, DC: National Defense University Press, 2011), p. 94.

[65] Lars S. Skålnes, *Politics, Markets, and Grand Strategy: Foreign Economic Policies As Strategic Instruments* (Ann Arbor, MI: University of Michigan Press, 2000).

[66] "KSA Gives $31 billion Aid to 78 Countries, Yemen Tops List," *Arab News*, June 22, 2018, www.arabnews.com/node/1325806/saudi-arabia;</int_u>; Nawaf Obaid, "Saudi Arabia Just Won Control of the Oil Market," *CNN*, March 20, 2020, www.cnn.com/2020/03/20/perspectives/saudi-arabia-oil-market/index.html.

[67] Carly West, "Qatar: Beyond the Blockade," *Global Risk Insights*, October 16, 2018, http://dehai.org/dehai/dehai-news/285309.

[68] "NOREF Methods," *Norwegian Center for Conflict Resolution,* (undated), https://noref.no/NOREF-methods#Track%20Two.

Cultural appeals can also play a significant role. Examples include those of great powers promoting education, like the Chinese Confucius Institutes or the US Fulbright program. The German building of Goethe Institutes and Saudi funding of madrassa throughout the Muslim world have also been influential.[69] A plethora of foundations and NGOs provide informal examples, including the work of organizations like the American Bar Association (promoting the rule of law) in Eastern Europe for two decades after the Cold War.[70] Proponents of the notion of soft power also add market-based elements to the list, such as movies and consumer goods, as part of the power of persuasion.[71]

There are negative counterparts. Sanctions have become widespread as a tool of economic statecraft in the twenty-first century.[72] The United States is exceptional in this regard because the financial system is largely denominated in US dollars, making the leverage exerted by its sanctions all the more powerful.[73] But other states can use their currencies by pegging it to the US dollar (almost three dozen did so in 2020).[74] Tariffs have often been used by states that have large domestic consumer markets, such as India. The denial of diplomatic recognition has played a role in Taiwan's development and, more generally, the weaponization of "Lawfare," defined by Charles Dunlap as "the use of regulation as an armament of conflict,"[75] has played an important strategic role

[69] Andrei S. Markovits and Simon Reich, *The German Predicament, Memory and Power in the New Europe* (Ithaca, NY: Cornell University Press, 1997), pp. 183–202; Carlo Jose Vincente Caro, "Fighting 'Radical Islamic Terrorism' Begins with Saudi Arabia," *The National Interest*, April 1, 2019, https://nationalinterest.org/blog/middle-east-watch/fighting-radical-islamic-terrorism-begins-saudi-arabia-50157.

[70] See "Ukraine (Past Program)," (undated), www.americanbar.org/advocacy/rule_of_law/where_we_work/europe_eurasia/ukraine/.

[71] For a discussion of this point, see Craig Hayden and Cynthia Schneider, "Captain America and Hip-Hop: American Soft Power Diplomacy," *Chicago Council on Global Affairs*, February 25, 2019, www.youtube.com/watch?v=1-jxHJb88lI.

[72] On sanctions, see Skålnes, *Politics, Markets, and Grand Strategy*; Brendan Taylor, "Sanctions As Grand Strategy," Adelphi Paper 411 (London: International Institute of Strategic Studies, 2010). On broader use of economic tools, see David Allen Baldwin, *Economic Statecraft* (Princeton, NJ: Princeton University Press, 1985).

[73] On the traditional role of the dollar, see Jonathan Kirshner, "Dollar Primacy and American Power: What's at Stake?," *Review of International Political Economy* 15, no. 3 (2008): pp. 418–438; For a discussion of the complex relationship and its consequences see "America's Aggressive Use of Sanctions Endangers the Dollar's Reign," *The Economist*, January 18, 2020, www.economist.com/briefing/2020/01/18/americas-aggressive-use-of-sanctions-endangers-the-dollars-reign.

[74] Scott Shpak, "What Currencies Are Pegged to the Dollar?," *Sapling*, (undated), www.sapling.com/4675892/what-currencies-pegged-dollar.

[75] Charles J. Dunlap Jr., "Law and Military Interventions: Preserving Humanitarian Values in 21st Century Conflicts," Harvard Carr Center working paper, November 29, 2001; see also Charles J. Dunlap Jr., "Lawfare Today: A Perspective," *Yale Journal of International Affairs* (Winter, 2008): pp. 146–154.

when used by the weak against the strong.[76] Threats of war or the use of armed force are the ultimate negative instruments. But again, warfare should not just be associated with great powers. Iran's engagement across the Middle East in Syria, Iraq and Yemen, and Saudi Arabia's response (notably in Yemen) are just two examples of regional powers employing military tools as part of their grand strategies.[77]

States therefore combine and configure this array of instruments differently as part of their grand strategies. The key questions concern which, when and how.

2.2.5 What Are the Available Resources (Means)?

Resources – the means – have to match the goals and instruments – the ends and ways – for a state to effectively implement a grand strategy.

Classicist scholars of grand strategy focus on the resources historically associated with the use of force. These generally include military materiel and its relationship to population size, economic productivity, natural resources (such as fossil fuels) and political capacity.[78] This approach can itself be interpreted narrowly, for example, by focusing on the capacity to build armaments for conventional warfare (such as iron or steel), or expansively on technological advantage (including the fighting of cyber wars). It can mean the size of a population or economy or the composition of either (such as the capacity for human capital or on metrics like GNP per capita rather than the absolute size of an economy).[79]

The resources associated with an IR definition are inevitably far more extensive, reflective of the diplomatic, informational, military and economic (DIME) list, in large part because the objectives linked with this version of grand

---

[76] Robert D. Williams, "Tribunal Issues Landmark Ruling in South China Sea Arbitration," *Lawfare*, July 12, 2016, www.lawfareblog.com/tribunal-issues-landmark-ruling-south-china-sea-arbitration.

[77] Seth Cropsey, "Iran's Grand Strategy: Gulf Crisis Keeps US from Helping Israel in a Two-Front War," *The Hill*, August 7, 2019, https://thehill.com/opinion/international/456496-irans-grand-strategy-gulf-crisis-keeps-us-from-helping-israel-in-a-two.

[78] See, for example, Ronald L. Tammen and Jacek Kugler, "Regional Challenge: China's Rise to Power" in *Asia-Pacific: A Region in Transition*, ed. Jim Rolfe (Honolulu: Asia-Pacific Center for Security Studies, 2004), p. 38. In explaining the metrics of political capacity, Tammen and Kugler assert (p. 41) that: "Politically capable governments have the capability of extracting resources from their populations; managing the economic productivity of individuals in their societies; and reducing birth rates in the early stages of development." In essence, a state's political capacity is therefore comprised of its organizational and extractive capabilities while maintaining domestic political stability. See also Ronald L. Tammen and Jacek Kugler, "Power Transition and China–US Conflicts," *Chinese Journal of International Politics* 1 (2006): pp. 35–55.

[79] Note that whether to focus on the total size of an economy or GDP per capita is central to the debate about Chinese and American economic capacity and possible American decline; Brooks and Wohlforth, *America Abroad*, pp. 31–39.

strategy can often be equally expansive. Brooks and Wohlforth, for example, cover some of the same ground as classicists but also emphasize as resources both economic (such as international or regional financial) institutions and military (such as formal, permanent alliance structures) institutions.[80] Yet their approach underlines the resources required to control or shape the global system, not to adapt to it.

Once adaptation is taken into account, the potential list of resources that may have utility for implementing a grand strategy proliferates. Substitutability, for example, can be a key ingredient in the economic domain. A surrogate for a fossil fuel capacity associated with a grand strategy, for example, can be sustainable forms of energy such as hydro or solar power, as Norway and Morocco respectively demonstrate.[81] Smaller states may not control the levers of the financial system, but they can wield enormous adaptive influence through their direction of massive sovereign wealth funds.[82]

Even the material resources associated with great powers are mirrored among smaller ones. As Brooks and Wohlforth note, an innovative technological base, built on human capital, allows for both military and civilian adaptation.[83] Israel demonstrates this point well.[84] Furthermore, the traditional domination of fossil fuel markets includes great powers (like Russia) but extends beyond them (notably, to Saudi Arabia). Having a national currency which a state can peg or devalue is a useful adaptive tool for exports, whether intended to offset a lack of competitiveness or address national poverty. Recognizing these as resources greatly helps to overcome the common misconception that a grand strategy requires a large bureaucracy and powerful military. The US huge foreign policy bureaucracy and its veto membership on the UN Security Council provides an enormously important resource in projecting diplomatic influence.[85] But small states can do the same through the UN or other means, as Norway has to promote equality and peace or Austria did as a bridge between East and West during the Cold War.[86]

---

[80] Ibid., pp. 2–3 and 15–46.
[81] Terje Osmundsen, "Norway's Renewables Exports to Increase 8-Fold by 2030," *Energypost.eu*, January 9, 2019, https://energypost.eu/norways-renewables-exports-to-increase-8-fold-by-2030/; Zafar, "Renewable Energy in Morocco."
[82] "Top 81 Largest Sovereign Wealth Fund Rankings by Total Assets," *Sovereign Wealth Fund Institute*, (undated), www.swfinstitute.org/fund-rankings/sovereign-wealth-fund.
[83] Brooks and Wohlforth, *America Abroad*, pp. 23–31.
[84] Shamir, "Israel," pp. 227, 230, 232.
[85] Joseph S. Nye, Jr., "Public Diplomacy and Soft Power," *The ANNALS of the American Academy of Political and Social Science* 616, no. 94 (2008): pp. 94–109, https://doi.org/10.1177/0002716207311699.
[86] David A. Cooper, "Challenging Contemporary Notions of Middle Power Influence: Implications of the Proliferation Security Initiative for 'Middle Power Theory'," *Foreign Policy Analysis* 7 (2011): pp. 317–336; Katarzyna Pisarska, "Peace Diplomacy and the Domestic Dimension of Norwegian Foreign Policy: The Insider's Accounts," *Scandinavian Political Studies* 38, no. 2

The diplomatic battle for "hearts and minds" is also a tool of grand strategy. It can take a variety of forms.[87] These include market-based cultural mechanisms stressing national values, like movies. An alternative is the use of media – both conventional such as the Voice of America, Al-Jezeera or Sputnik Radio, or social such as the strategic use of disinformation campaigns. Finally, often independent from the state but consistent with its goals is the work of some NGOs and foundations. These are often associated with Western values and agencies of the state in their promotion of equity, free speech and the rule of law.[88]

In sum, grand strategic resources are far more varied than a Realist focus on military capacities suggests. Even broader Liberal variants incorporating soft forms of power are too limited: first, because they conceive of using such resources only in the process of controlling or shaping rather than adapting; and, second, because they ignore the fact that small states also have these resources or can effectively employ substitutable resources.

2.2.6 Which Kinds of Threats or Opportunities Does a Grand Strategy Prioritize?

Grand strategies differentiate between kinds of threats. First, some focus predominantly on traditional national security kinetic threats, primarily conventional and nuclear warfare that dominated during the Cold War, when deterrence or compellence, managing allies and fighting proxy wars were the substance of grand strategy. Asymmetric (such as terrorism) or hybrid (including cyber and disinformation) forms of warfare have complicated that relatively simple calculus. But the principle of this approach reflects the belief that, "Grand strategy is ultimately about fighting."[89] Michele Flournoy argues, however, that this definition may be too narrow when considering national security and, by implication, the purpose of a grand strategy.[90] A broader definition applicable to many states could include two variations already briefly mentioned.

(January 21, 2015), https://doi.org/10.1111/1467-9477.12042; Carmen Gebhard, "Is Small Still Beautiful? The Case of Austria," *Swiss Political Science Review* 19, no. 3, pp. 279–297. On track two diplomacy, see Dalia Dassa Kaye, "Talking to the Enemy: Track Two Diplomacy in the Middle East and South Asia," Rand Corporation (2007), www.rand.org/content/dam/rand/pubs/monographs/2007/RAND_MG592.pdf.

[87] Ben D. Mor, "Public Diplomacy in Grand Strategy," *Foreign Policy Analysis* 2 (2006), pp. 157–176.

[88] Don Melvin, "Russia Bans 'Undesirable' NGOs, Sparking International Outcry," *CNN*, May 24, 2015, www.cnn.com/2015/05/24/europe/russia-bans-undesirable-ngos/index.html; Krisztina Than, "Civil Organizations in Hungary Brace for Government Crackdown on NGOs," *Reuters*, April 25, 2018, www.reuters.com/article/us-hungary-orban-ngos/civil-organizations-in-hungary-brace-for-government-crackdown-on-ngos-idUSKBN1HW1ZN.

[89] Posen, *Restraint*, p. 1.

[90] Aaron Mehta, "Public Health Must Be Part of National Security Calculus, Says Flournoy," *Defense News*, March 27, 2020, www.defensenews.com/news/coronavirus/2020/03/26/public-health-must-be-part-of-national-security-calculus-says-former-defense-official/.

The first includes anthropogenic threats – those inadvertently made by humans that have malicious effects but are not the product of malicious intent. Climate change provides the most significant contemporary example. Neither states nor corporations intend to choke the environment as a goal when they generate CO_2 or illicitly dispose of insecticide, despoiling collective goods such as air or water. Yet these pollutants generate problems for states, both individually and collectively. The same is broadly true of food and water insecurity. Water sources are often not club goods, their source being shared by potential or actual enemies such as India and Pakistan. Food resources, however, are often rivalrous and competitive, particularly in wartime.[91]

The second type of threats are naturogenic. They emanate from nature, often with devastating effects. The Spanish Flu in the second decade of the twentieth century reputedly killed fifty million people globally (including 675,000 Americans) and was long regarded as the benchmark for pandemics in the modern world. Avian influenza, Ebola, H1N1, Middle East respiratory syndrome coronavirus (MERS-CoV), severe acute respiratory syndrome (SARS) and Zika all provided warnings of the potential effects of viruses in the twenty-first century. These warnings were sufficient for the US intelligence community's worldwide threat assessment to include pandemics and other health hazards every year between 2009 and 2016.[92]

Realists dismiss these threats as beyond the purview of grand strategy. Consistent with that approach, the US Department of Defense routinely failed to integrate these concerns into strategic planning.[93] Yet criticism of such positions as hyperbole or irrelevant – in terms of the devastating casualty, economic or social effects – has been disproved in the context of the spread of COVID-19.[94] By February 2021, it was projected to soon surpass the number of Americans killed in combat during World War I, World War II, the Korean War and Vietnam Wars combined (more than 500,000 deaths). As Flournoy

---

[91] Fen Osler Hampson with Jean Daudelin, John B. Hay, Todd Martin and Holly Reid, *Madness in the Multitude: Human Security and World Disorder* (New York: Oxford University Press, 2002), pp. 38–40.

[92] GAO, "Defense Civil Support: DOD, HHS, and DHS Should Use Existing Coordination Mechanisms to Improve Their Pandemic Preparedness" (Washington, DC: Government Accountability Office, 2017); National Academies of Sciences, Engineering, and Medicine, Health and Medicine Division, Board on Global Health, "Global Health and the Future Role of the United States" (Washington, DC: National Academies Press,2017), www.ncbi.nlm.nih.gov /books/NBK458470/.

[93] Simon Reich and Peter Dombrowksi, "The Consequence of COVID-19: How the United States Moved from Security Provider to Security Consumer," *International Affairs* 96, no. 5, pp. 1253–1279, https://academic.oup.com/ia/article/96/5/1253/5901375.

[94] Ronald Brownstein, "Why Trump Wants to Be Seen As a 'Wartime' President," *CNN*, March 24, 2020, www.cnn.com/2020/03/24/politics/fault-lines-trump-coronavirus-wartime-president /index.html.

notes, "Dealing with pandemics and safeguarding the health of the American population from a threat like [coronavirus] should be part of our national security thinking and rubric ... We have got to think about public health preparedness as part of our national security going forward."[95]

These threats all share a common transnational feature. Indeed, the illicit global flows of arms and fissile materials, drugs, people, money and technology (including intellectual property rights theft) have all become the substance of national security.[96] Even job security, unfair trade, human trafficking and migration have been redefined as national security issues in major government reports.[97] All have become the legitimate focus of grand strategies.

According to the classical approach, opportunities are generally narrowly defined in terms of an immediate military advantage. Leverage is a product of an opponent's weaknesses, such as resource denial through the choking of supply lines, which often employs sea power.[98] China's reliance on imported oil, for example, may provide other states with the opportunity to close the Malacca Strait in the event of war (as discussed in section 5). China's response is to build overland supply capabilities – through the Belt and Road Initiative – to address this possible hazard.[99]

Liberal grand strategists, however, often orient strategic opportunities in terms of incentives. This approach may be illustrated by the extension of NATO membership after 1991, when so many former Warsaw Pact countries clambered to be admitted; or the EU's expansion program which admitted eight central and eastern European countries on May 1, 2004. This has relevance for great powers, such as the offer to trade China its "market economy status" at the World Trade Organization in exchange for political or market reforms.[100] Alternatively, opportunities may focus on longer-term considerations, emblematic in the construction of global institutions such as China's recent creation of the multilateral Asian

---

[95] Quoted in Mehta, "Public health."

[96] Moisés Naim, "The Five Wars of Globalization," *Foreign Policy*, November 3, 2009, https://foreignpolicy.com/2009/11/03/five-wars-of-globalization/.

[97] See, for example, the 2015 *National Security Strategy*, pp. 12, 13, 15 and the *2017 National Security Strategy*, p. 1.

[98] Paul M. Kennedy, *The Rise and Fall of British Naval Mastery* (London: Macmillan, 1983 [first published by Allen Lane in 1976]; Alfred Thayer Mahan, *The Influence of Sea Power Upon History, 1660–1783* (Project Gutenberg, e-book), www.gutenberg.org/files/13529/13529-h/13529-h.htm.

[99] Andrew Chatzky and James McBride, "China's Massive Belt and Road Initiative," *Council on Foreign Relations*, January 28, 2020, www.cfr.org/backgrounder/chinas-massive-belt-and-road-initiative; "How Is China's Energy Footprint Changing," *Chinapower*, March 19, 2020, https://chinapower.csis.org/energy-footprint.

[100] The Trump administration opposed that initiative in 2017, allowing the United States to maintain anti-dumping duties on China and use its absence as leverage in trade negotiations; David Lawder, "US Formally Opposes China Market Economy Status at WTO," *Reuters*, November 30, 2017, www.reuters.com/article/us-usa-china-trade-wto/u-s-formally-opposes-china-market-economy-status-at-wto-idUSKBN1DU2VH.

Table 1 A framework for comparing grand strategies

Definition:	Classical	v. International relations	
Scope:	Global	v. Regional	v. Local
Assumptions	Homogenous	v. Heterogenous actors	
	Zero	v. Positive Sum Relationship	
Purpose:	Control, shape, adapt, detach		
Degree of Strategic Coordination:	Unilateral, bilateral, multilateral		
Ends:	Create or sustain advantage		
	Address historic injustice		
	Restore imperial status		
	Recognize as a normal state		
Ways:	Diplomatic domain:	Role in international organizations, bilateral negotiation, Exchange Programs, Cultural Promotion Denial or according of diplomatic recognition	
	Military domain:	Combat deployment and exercises Training and materiel assistance	
	Economic domain:	Aid, preferential market/trade access finance agreements, currency floating and pegging sanctions, tariffs, austerity measures, intellectual property rights development and/or theft.	
Means:	Military Domain:	Conventional War materiel, nuclear weaponry, population size and demographics, cyber capacity	
	Economic Domain:	Technological innovation capacity, size of GDP, GDP per capita, access to natural resources, control of domestic and global market access for essential natural and technological resources, global role of currency, access to lending/capital markets, sovereign wealth funds.	
	Diplomatic Domain:	Representation in regional and global forums, recognized influence in multilateral and bilateral forums, statecraft in negotiations	
Threats:	Kinetic:	Conventional, nuclear, asymmetric, hybrid/cyber	
	Anthropogenic:	Climate, environmental, food and water security,	
	Naturogenic:	Global health, pandemics, biosecurity	
Opportunities:	Military:	Predatory: Adaptive or tactical	
	Economic:	Institution building, market leadership, technological advantage	
	Diplomatic:	Cultural assimilation and diplomatic recognition	

Infrastructure Investment Bank to fund its Belt and Road Initiative, with 102 approved members including many American allies.[101]

Seizing grand strategic opportunities is not only the province of great powers. Initiatives in developing human capital related to digitalization (Singapore and Estonia), sustainable solar capacity (Morocco), an aviation hub (UAE), an educational hub (Dubai) or several of these elements combined (Rwanda) are formulated and implemented as grand strategies.[102] It is a refusal to recognize them as such, rather than their absence, which blinds us to their existence.

2.3 Conclusion

The framework we have presented provides for significant variation in terms of national grand strategies. We present a summary version of our discussion in Table 1 on page 22.

Our framework is neither a model nor a theory. Rather, it attempts to recognize and capture the varied options that states face in formulating and implementing a grand strategy. They can be – and are – combined in a myriad of ways. That is why (as we discuss in the next section) there are several variants of types of Realist grand strategy. And that is why national grand strategies can change over time. The way these choices configure, in the context of one state's choices, allows for comparison – across type, time and space.

In section 3 we examine how the clustering of those choices are reflected in the different types of grand strategies that are commonly debated among academics analyzing American grand strategies.

3. Types of Grand Strategy

Typologies have practical purposes. They commonly describe ideal types.[103] But comparing them also acts as a basis for theory building, allowing us to transparently, systematically understand what is distinct about each type.[104] This includes identifying the unacknowledged assumptions of the kind discussed in section 2 – alerting us to their presence, allowing us to evaluate their

---

[101] Asian Infrastructure Investment Bank, "Who We Are," (undated), https://www.aiib.org/en/about-aiib/index.html.

[102] See Claver Gatete, "The Rwanda We Want: Towards Vision 2050," (Minister of Finance and Economic Planning, Rwanda, National Dialogue Presentation, December 16, 2016), www.minecofin.gov.rw/fileadmin/user_upload/Hon_Gatete_Umushyikirano_Presentation_2016.pdf.

[103] On confusion regarding their purpose, see Jon Hendricks and C. Breckinridge Peters, "The Ideal Type and Sociological Theory," *Acta Sociologica* 16, no. 1, 1973, pp. 31–40.

[104] On the use of heuristics in case studies, see Harry Eckstein, "Case Study and Theory in Political Science" in *Handbook of Political Science VII*, eds. Fred I. Greenstein and Nelson W. Polsby (Reading, MA: Addison-Wesley, 1975), especially pp. 106–107. For a discussion of the role of heuristics in theory building, see Herbert A. Simon, *The Sciences of the Artificial* (Cambridge, MA: MIT Press, 3rd edition, 1996).

internal consistency and providing an opportunity to assess their theoretical and policy implications. Constructing types also provides a tool for developing the causative relationships so often lacking in scholarship on grand strategy.[105] As Peer Fiss notes, typologies and causality are intrinsically related.[106] Scholars often compare primarily for the purpose of prescribing their preferred formulation, generating accusations of bias. This happens repeatedly in the field of grand strategy, where scholars speak to the "pros" of their position and the "cons" of others.[107] The few typologies that have been offered show bias in favor of the classical definition that emphasizes the militarized aspects of grand strategy, omitting forms that emphasize other purposes or tools.

Bearing these tendencies in mind, we undertake two tasks in this section. First, we examine the grand strategy typologies that have been developed to date and explain their limitations. We then apply the framework laid out in section 2 to five distinct types of US grand strategy that span both classical and IR definitions. This breadth captures a spectrum of options that overwhelmingly compete for attention among American scholars and policymakers. But, as we will attempt to demonstrate in section 5, there are elements that can be applied to other states.

3.1 Enduring and Recent Typologies in the field of Grand Strategy

Barry Posen and Andrew Ross's two-decade-old formulation remains a remarkably resilient benchmark.[108] They present four types. Three are variants of Realism – primacy, selective engagement and neo-isolationism. The fourth is a Liberal variant – cooperative security. Posen and Ross offer no definition of a grand strategy.[109] However, the central questions they ask about each approach, the policy instruments they examine and the application of their analysis to policy questions leaves no doubt that they employed a classical definition. Their framework offers several conceptual categories (such as contending definitions of the national interest) and an implicit reference

---

[105] Mattei Dogan and Dominique Pelassy, *How to Compare Nations: Strategies in Comparative Politics* (Washington, DC: CQ Press, 1990), pp. 151–154; John Lofland and Lyn H. Lofland, *Analyzing Social Settings* (Belmont, CA: Wadsworth, 3rd edition, 1995); and Martyn Hammersley and Paul Atkinson, *Ethnography: Principles in Practice* (London: Routledge 2nd edition, 1995), pp. 172–174.

[106] Peer C. Fiss, "Building Better Causal Theories: A Fuzzy Set Approach to Typologies in Organizational Research," *Academy of Management Journal* 54, no. 2 (2011): p. 393, https://pdfs.semanticscholar.org/d0eb/fa45ee8b607177bec0e101b342b1a42fbdda.pdf,

[107] Kevin Narizny, "American Grand Strategy and Political Economy Theory" in *Oxford Research Encyclopedia of Politics*, ed. William R. Thompson (Oxford: Oxford University Press, 2017), pp. 1–24.

[108] Barry R. Posen and Andrew L. Ross, "Competing Visions for U.S. Grand Strategy," *International Security* 21, no. 3 (Winter, 1996/97), pp. 5–53.

[109] Posen subsequently settled on "a grand strategy is a nation-state's theory of how to produce security for itself" in Posen, *Restraint*, p. 1.

to prevailing theories (what they term "preferred world order"). But they lay far greater emphasis on each variant's application in specific policy areas – nuclear proliferation, NATO, ethnic conflict and humanitarian intervention.[110]

Other authors have offered subsequent typologies. Peter Layton, for example, notes a tripod of denial, engagement and reform grand strategies, entailing different balances of military, economic and diplomatic power. It is a potentially useful distinction but lacks the systematic framework that can be explored comparatively.[111] Paul Avey, Jonathan Markowitz and Robert Reardon have more recently offered an updated version of Posen and Ross's typology. Their classification's value-added is evident in comparing some well-known contemporary strategies: restraint, deep engagement, liberal internationalism and conservative primacy. Yet, their focus on conventional national security, and curious omission of some variant of isolationism in the context of the Trump administration, is especially puzzling.[112]

So, why have a new typology? Posen and Ross avow that, "Our purpose is not advocacy; it is transparency."[113] Echoing that spirit, we offer two justifications for our alternative typology. First, their version's vintage means that it does not include adaptive variants of grand strategy that have emerged and been used by successive American administrations. The most obvious example we present is that of sponsorship, often disparaged as "leading from behind."[114] It seeks to limit strategic commitments yet legitimate American operations by abandoning a hegemonic position in favor of selectively accepting international law and norms as the basis for action in addressing collective action problems. Posen and Ross did not anticipate an option employed by successive presidents in the twenty-first century.[115]

Second, the utility of some of the formulations that Posen and Ross did examine has declined in the last two decades because they were more relevant in a Cold War context – notably, conventional interstate conflict in Europe.[116] This classical bias is further reflected in their emphasis on both the "use of force" and "force posture" as categories. Interstate conflict has precipitously declined

---

[110] Posen and Ross, "Competing Visions for U.S. Grand Strategy," p. 4 (table 1). Some prominent scholars have subsequently rejected these types and collapsed grand strategies into a twofold distinction between "liberal hegemony" and restraint. See, John J. Mearsheimer, *The Great Delusion: Liberal Dreams and International Realities* (New Haven, CT: Yale University Press, 2018).

[111] Peter Layton, *Grand Strategy* (self-published, 2018).

[112] Avey, Markowitz and Reardon, "Disentangling Grand Strategy."

[113] Posen and Ross, "Competing Visions for U.S. Grand Strategy," p. 3.

[114] Josh Rogin, "Who Really Said Obama Was 'leading from behind'?" *Foreign Policy*, October 27, 2011, https://foreignpolicy.com/2011/10/27/who-really-said-obama-was-leading-from-behind/.

[115] Peter Dombrowski and Simon Reich, "The Strategy of Sponsorship," *Survival* 57, no. 5, (October/November, 2015) pp. 121–148.

[116] See Posen and Ross, "Competing Visions for U.S. Grand Strategy," p. 4 (table 1).

and their fourfold formulation is uncomfortably suited to a security environment where the existential threats have expanded to include new forms of kinetic, anthropogenic and naturogenic challenges. Asserting that grand strategy should be confined to conventional national security is unjustified when compared with legitimate public concerns, realistic threats and data on the most common forms of armed conflict today.[117] This disjuncture is reflected in a succession of US *National Security Strategy* reports, where conventional and nuclear war constitute a diminishing part of the agenda. Prominent national security issues now include terrorism, the proliferation of weapons of mass destruction and cyber warfare. They also extend in official documents to economic insecurity, trafficking, climate change and global health threats.[118]

3.2 Five Competing Formulations

We now present five formulations of grand strategy by addressing the questions outlined in section 2. Some answers to some framing questions are superficially identical across types, while others remain distinct. The outcome, however, is that each variant of a grand strategy has a unique configuration and balances the use of instruments in contrasting ways (see Table 2 and Table 3 in section 3.3).

3.2.1 Primacy

Definition and Scope

As Benjamin Friedman and Justin Logan wrote in 2016, "[t]he vast majority of US foreign policy makers are devotees of primacy, a grand strategy that sees global US military exertions—alliances, foreign bases, patrols, military training, regular wars, and continual airstrikes—as the only guarantee of national security, global stability, and free trade."[119] Posen and Ross capture the vast

---

[117] Posen, *Restraint*, p. 1. For a data overview on armed conflicts, see Watson Institute, Brown University, Costs of War Project, https://watson.brown.edu/costsofwar/. For polling data on climate change, see Brian Kennedy and Meg Hefferon, "U.S. Concern about Climate Change Is Rising, but Mainly among Democrats," Pew Research Center, August 28, 2019, www.pewresearch.org/fact-tank/2019/08/28/u-s-concern-about-climate-change-is-rising-but-mainly-among-democrats/.

[118] George W. Bush focused on human trafficking in *National Security Strategy of the United States of America 2006* (Washington, DC: The White House, March, 2006), p. 7, www.comw.org/qdr/full text/nss2006.pdf; Obama highlighted health issues, infectious diseases and the Millennium Development Goals in *National Security Strategy of the United States 2015* (Washington, DC: The White House, February, 2015), pp. 2, 17, https://obamawhitehouse.archives.gov/sites/default/files/docs/2015_national_security_strategy_2.pdf; and Trump emphasized crime, jobs and drugs in *National Security Strategy of the United States of America 2017* (Washington, DC: The White House, December, 2017), p.1, https://www.hsdl.org/?view&did=806478.

[119] Benjamin H. Friedman and Justin Logan, "Why Washington Doesn't Debate Grand Strategy," *Strategic Studies Quarterly* 10, no. 4 (Winter, 2016), pp. 14.

scope of the primacist position in suggesting that they seek to "preserve US supremacy by politically, economically, and militarily outdistancing any global challenger."[120] As the draft 1992 Defense Planning Guidance noted, the post–Cold War US strategy "must now refocus on precluding the emergence of any potential future global competitor."[121] The Trump administration returned to this theme – the rise of revisionist powers – in its 2017 *National Security Strategy*.[122] Primacy in the extreme may even entail the sacrifice of other domestic and international goals (e.g. fiscal solvency, American values, and settled international law) in the service of dominance. As Christopher Lane diagnosed it, "[w]ith respect to U.S. commitments, the strategy of preponderance is open-ended."[123]

While expansive, both geographically and in ambition, primacy nonetheless construes the purpose of grand strategy narrowly. Domination entails military advantage built upon a foundation of resource and technological capacity, employing a classical definition of grand strategy. For many, primacy endures – with significant success. Hal Brands suggests,

> on balance, it helped ensure that the post-Cold War system has so far been more stable, more liberal, and more congenial to U.S. interests than many leading observers predicted a quarter-century ago . . . The time has not come for radical retrenchment; the proper course, rather, is to do what is necessary to sustain the grand strategy that America has pursued, more or less successfully, over the past quarter century.[124]

Underlying Assumptions

Primacists assume that competition is endemic to the international system, indeed to political life. Samuel Huntington claimed, "Competition – the struggle for primacy – we all recognize as natural among individuals, corporations, political parties, athletes, and universities; it is no less natural among countries."[125] The US, he asserted, is indispensable: "The maintenance of U.S. primacy matters for the world as well as for the United States," because

---

[120] Posen and Ross, "Competing Visions for U.S. Grand Strategy" p. 32.

[121] "Excerpts From Pentagon's Plan: 'Prevent the Re-Emergence of a New Rival'," *New York Times*, March 8, 1992, www.nytimes.com/1992/03/08/world/excerpts-from-pentagon-s-plan-prevent-the-re-emergence-of-a-new-rival.html.

[122] *National Security Strategy of the United States of America 2017*, p. 25.

[123] Christopher Layne, "From Preponderance to Offshore Balance: America's Future Grand Strategy," *International Security* 22, no. 1 (Summer, 1997), p. 101.

[124] Hal Brands, "The Pretty Successful Superpower," *National Interest*, November 14, 2016, www.the-american-interest.com/2016/11/14/the-pretty-successful-superpower/.

[125] Samuel P. Huntington, "Why International Primacy Matters," *International Security* 17, no. 4 (Spring, 1993), p. 69. See also Richard N. Haass, *The Reluctant Sheriff: The United States after the Cold War* (New York: Council on Foreign Relations Press, 1997); Michael Mandelbaum,

"no other country can make comparable contributions to international order and stability."[126] According to Brooks and Wohlforth, American material resources remain sufficient to maintain pre-eminence even in the face of emerging great power challengers for many decades to come.[127] At worst, Robert Lieber suggests, "to the extent that limits to American primacy do exist, they are just as likely to be ideational as they are material. The problem inheres as much or more in elite and societal beliefs and policy choices, as in economic, technological or manpower limitations at home, or the rise of peer competitors abroad."[128] The key ingredients, beyond resources, are political will and leadership.

Geostrategic Objectives ("Ends")

Primacists want to command the global system. They seek, "the creation and maintenance of a U.S.-led world order based on preeminent U.S. political, military, and economic power, and on American values; maximization of U.S. control over the international system by preventing the emergence of rival great powers in Europe and East Asia; and maintenance of economic interdependence as a vital U.S. security interest."[129] Some, further, advocate using primacy to spread American values and institutions to reinforce and sustain the material foundations of its global power. As Colin Dueck observes, they "genuinely believe that America's democratic and free market values can be promoted successfully worldwide."[130] William Kristol and Robert Kagan, for example, argued that:

> the enormous disparity between U.S. military strength and that of any potential challenger is a good thing for America and the world. After all, America's world role is entirely different from that of the other powers. The more Washington is able to make clear that it is futile to compete with American power, either in size of forces or in technological capabilities, the less chance there is that countries like China or Iran will entertain ambitions of upsetting the present world order.[131]

The Case for Goliath: How America Acts As the World's Government in the Twenty-First Century (New York: Public Affairs, 2005).

[126]	Huntington, "Why International Primacy Matters," p. 82.

[127]	Brooks and Wohlforth, *America Abroad,* see especially chapters 2 and 3.

[128]	Robert J. Lieber, "Staying Power and the American Future: Problems of Primacy, Policy, and Grand Strategy," *Journal of Strategic Studies* 34, no. 4 (2011), p. 510.

[129]	Christopher Layne, "From Preponderance to Offshore Balance," p. 89.

[130]	Colin Dueck, "Ideas and Alternatives in American Grand Strategy, 2000–2004," *Review of International Studies* 30, no. 4 (October, 2004), p. 516.

[131]	William Kristol and Robert Kagan, "Toward a Neo-Reaganite Foreign Policy," *Foreign Affairs* 75, no.18 (1996), p. 26.

The "Ways"

Huntington argued that: "Primacy is desirable not primarily to achieve victory in war but to achieve the state's goals without recourse to war."[132] Yet, the dominant strand relies heavily on the use of military strength. As Nuno Monteiro explains, "primacy involves the unipole's regular use of military force to further its interests."[133] Karl Eikenberry notes that America's recourse to military action has accelerated over time: The military was used in 19 military deployments between 1946 and 1973 but expanded to 144 between 1974 and 2013.[134]

The Instruments ("Means")

Conventional military superiority requires power projection capabilities and the ability to control the global commons. This entails a large conventional, expeditionary army well supplied with main battle tanks, artillery and tactically mobile helicopters. It also requires a fleet of maritime and air transports to deploy army brigades. Transport must have a navy and air force with the ability to protect and defend air, land and sea lines of communication, while having sufficient bombs and missiles available to attack targets anywhere, anytime. Underpinning this capacity is a global system of military bases, logistics and communications infrastructures, space and other intelligence, surveillance and reconnaissance systems supported by a robust defense industrial sector.

Conventional military superiority is augmented by nuclear supremacy. According to Keir Lieber and Daryl Press, "The intentional pursuit of nuclear primacy is, moreover, entirely consistent with the United States' declared policy of expanding its global dominance."[135] The United States has thus pursued nuclear modernization, the development of new nuclear weapons and delivery systems, and national and regional missile defense systems.[136] Superiority requires unremitting effort.

---

[132] Huntington, "Why International Primacy Matters," p. 72.

[133] Nuno P. Monteiro, "Assured: Why Unipolarity Is Not Peaceful," *International Security* 36, no. 3 (Winter, 2011/12), p. 14, footnote 36.

[134] Karl W. Eikenberry, "The Militarization of US Foreign Policy," *American Foreign Policy Interests* 35 (2013), pp. 1–8, http://dx.doi.org/10.1080/10803920.2013.757952; see also Gordon Adams and Shoon Murray, eds., *Mission Creep: The Militarization of US Foreign Policy?* (Washington, DC: Georgetown University Press 2014).

[135] Keir A. Lieber and Daryl G. Press, "The Rise of U.S. Nuclear Primacy," *Foreign Affairs* 85, no. 2 (March/April, 2006), p. 52.

[136] Catherine McArdle Kelleher and Peter Dombrowski, eds., *Regional Missile Defense from a Global Perspective* (Palo Alto, CA: Stanford University Press 2015).

The Threats and Opportunities

Primacists prioritize thwarting the rise of peer competitors. This was a theoretical challenge in the 1990s, albeit it one that George H. W. Bush's administration recognized in draft defense planning documents.[137] China's subsequent economic and military growth, coupled with Russia's aggression, has convinced many American strategists that this challenge is no longer purely theoretical. The Trump administration's strategic documents, with their focus on great power rivalry with China and Russia, now dominates the Washington national security discourse despite Trump's departure from office.[138]

An intellectual basis for this concern is power transition theory in which a rising challenger, eventually disgruntled with existing constraining rules, seeks to overturn the existing order through great power war against a declining hegemon. The disparity between relative power distribution and the dysfunctional logistical organization of the global system becomes the basis for war.[139] This threat is augmented by concerns about other potential adversaries aligning – bandwagoning – with a rising power.[140] Signs of a declining relative military advantage, or of any of the capacities that sustain that advantage – natural resources, population size, the size of an economy and political capacity – generate great anguish among primacists.[141] Indeed, America periodically debates the prospect of decline or renewal.

Primacy axiomatically entails an unending global commitment. A limit on resources generates an inevitable tension between the focus on peer competitors and a tendency to assert US interests and preferences wherever its dominance may be challenged. Friedman and Logan argue that "[p]rimacy's advocates see many threats to the United States" including actions that weaken the "credibility of the many promises the United States makes to defend allies" and "the proliferation of weapons technology, especially nuclear weapons"; even "internal conditions abroad (foreign civil wars, failed states, or illiberal governments) can easily undermine US global leadership."[142] This view has resulted in

---

[137] Zalmay Khalilzad, *From Containment to Global Leadership? America and the World After the Cold War* (Santa Monica, CA: RAND, 1995).

[138] *National Security Strategy of the United States of America 2017*; US Department of Defense, *Summary of the 2018 National Defense Strategy of the United States of America*, www.hsdl.org /?view&did=807329.

[139] Henk Houweling and Jan G. Siccama, "Power Transitions as a Cause of War," *The Journal of Conflict Resolution* 32, no. 1 (1988): pp. 87–102; A. F. K. Organski, *World Politics* (New York: Knopf, 1958); Ronald L. Tammen and Jacek Kugler, "Power Transition and China–U.S. Conflicts," *Chinese Journal of International Politics* 1, no. 1 (2006): pp. 35–55.

[140] Stephen M. Walt, *The Origins of Alliances* (Ithaca, NY: Cornell University Press, 1987).

[141] Ronald L. Tammen and Jacek Kugler, "Regional Challenge: China's Rise to Power," in *Asia-Pacific: A Region in Transition*, ed. Jim Rolfe (Honolulu: Asia-Pacific Center for Security Studies, 2004), pp. 33–53.

[142] Friedman and Logan, "Why Washington Doesn't Debate Grand Strategy," p. 18.

increased defense budgets to readjust American military forces to meet a never-ending set of commitments.[143]

Opportunities are narrowly construed as locating vulnerabilities in challengers that can be exploited for relative gain. These most cogently relate to the correlation of forces but can be extended to underlying technological or raw material resources.

3.2.2 Deep Engagement

Definition and Scope

Advocates have argued that deep engagement has been the United States' de facto position since 1945, although even they debate its meaning. One position is that it consists of multilateral diplomatic, economic and military leadership; another, deep engagement *plus*, is that it extends to the promotion of democracy, human rights and, effectively, humanitarian intervention.[144] Both positions, however, share the view that benign American preeminence has stabilized the global liberal order and generated shared benefits.

Deep engagement embraces an IR definition of grand strategy with a broad scope, balancing American multilateral leadership in diplomatic, economic and military domains. As Brooks, Ikenberry and Wohlforth contend, "In an effort to protect its security and prosperity, the country has promoted a liberal economic order and established close defense ties with partners in Europe, East Asia, and the Middle East."[145] The US thus assumes global responsibility for both a negotiated economic system and an institutionalized, rules-based defense commitment but, when necessary, reduces that geographic scope to these three key regions.[146] Although not an advocate of deep engagement, as Art notes, focusing on key regions "avoids both an overly restrictive and an overly expansive definition of America's interests, and it strikes a balance between doing too much and too little militarily to support them."[147] The Trump administration's policies, which weakened that liberal order, led to concerns that the US itself was eviscerating important institutional underpinnings.[148]

---

[143] Gordon Adams and Cindy Williams, *Buying National Security: How America Plans and Pays for Its Global Role and Safety at Home* (New York: Routledge, 2010).

[144] Brooks and Wohlforth, *America Abroad*, p. 73.

[145] Stephen G. Brooks, G. John Ikenberry, and William C. Wohlforth, "Lean Forward: In Defense of American Engagement," *Foreign Affairs* 2, no. 130 (2013): p. 130.

[146] Ibid.

[147] Robert J. Art, "Geopolitics Updated: A Strategy of Selective Engagement," *International Security* 23, no. 3 (Winter, 1998/99): p. 80.

[148] G. John Ikenberry, "The End of the Liberal International Order?," *International Affairs* 94, no. 1, (2018): pp. 7-23, https://doi.org/10.1093/ia/iix241.

Underlying Assumptions

All proponents of deep engagement assume the virtues of US global leadership, believing that "military power underwrites an open economic order"[149] and that its leadership requires deep engagement.[150] Furthermore, "sustaining a global presence enables systematic use of soft balancing–style tools to restrain and shape others' behavior."[151] The theoretical justification for this belief stems from a benign version of hegemonic stability theory, whereby a network of institutionalized security agreements yields mutual benefits to the United States and other states.[152] Gains are therefore absolute and positive-sum. Others may therefore garner benefits too. But aggregate benefits to the United States – stability and prosperity – justify these costs.[153] Deep engagement thus requires that the United States possesses the resources necessary to sustain military and economic linkages across the globe.[154] Advocates call this leadership. Critics call it controlling.

Geostrategic Objectives

Proponents claim that the liberal order has enabled unprecedented economic growth, a long peace free from great power conflict, and allowed the "West" to contain and then vanquish the Soviet challenge. They recognize the difficulties of systems maintenance associated with relative American decline, challengers to American preponderance (for example, China), and the multipolarity associated with the "rise of the rest." But they respond that the system must endure.[155] The United States should maintain the status quo because it has the material resources and political influence to do so. They believe that "international institutions can 'lock in' rules and norms that will continue to reflect U.S. interests even after the United States' relative power advantage has declined."[156] Although anxious about the Trump administration's policies, they regarded the undermining of the liberal order as an aberration requiring adjustment rather than a fundamental change.[157]

---

[149] Norrlof and Wohlforth, "Is US Grand Strategy Self-Defeating?," p. 230.

[150] Joseph Nye, "East Asian Security: The Case for Deep Engagement," *Foreign Affairs* 74, no. 4 (July/August, 1995): pp. 96–101.

[151] Stephen G. Brooks, G. John Ikenberry and William C. Wohlforth, "Don't Come Home America: The Case against Retrenchment," *International Security* 37, no. 3 (Winter, 2012/13): pp. 23–24.

[152] Robert Keohane, *After Hegemony: Cooperation and Discord in the World Political Economy* (Princeton, NJ: Princeton University Press, 1984).

[153] Brooks, Ikenberry, and Wohlforth, "Don't Come Home America," pp. 32–41.

[154] Brooks and Wohlforth, *America Abroad.*

[155] Ibid., p. 4.

[156] Evan Braden Montgomery, "Contested Primacy in the Western Pacific: China's Rise and the Future of U.S. Power Projection," *International Security* 38, no. 4 (Spring, 2014): footnote 9.

[157] Ikenberry, "The End of the Liberal International Order?," pp. 8–9.

The "Ways"

Avey, Markowitz and Reardon suggest that "[s]upporters of deep engagement seek to construct a military capable of maintaining existing alliance commitments and troop deployments abroad."[158] The American military response to any threat must be tailored to specific circumstances. China's military modernization, for example, entails a focus on anti-access/area denial systems and geographic advantages in the Asian littoral.[159] The American military must therefore place "a much greater emphasis on air and undersea platforms that can survive inside nonpermissive environments, forward bases that are better able to withstand attacks, and information networks that are less vulnerable to disruption."[160]

Proponents accept the costs, benefits and responsibilities associated with the long-standing bilateral and multilateral alliances, particularly NATO. As Brooks, Ikenberry and Wohlforth argue, "The result is to make the U.S. alliance system—especially among its core liberal members—far more robust and harder to challenge than if the United States were to disengage."[161] This requires that the United States maintains a forward presence, relying on overseas military bases and forces, while supporting regional institutions.[162]

"How" to restrain adversaries is unclear, although both negotiation and institutionalization are key ingredients. A domestic consensus in support of deep engagement and bearing costs to realize greater benefits is fundamental. American leaders must therefore "arrive at a more selective grand strategy that enjoys broad domestic support than to continue drifting toward an intractable polarization that is a recipe for political stalemate at home and failed leadership abroad."[163] For that to succeed, the American economy must remain robust and the state's ability to borrow to pay for the liberal order must be unhindered.

The Instruments ("Means")

Deep engagement entails expending America's resources liberally. Debates between deep engagers and their critics center on the costs and returns on investment. Advocates believe it affordable and deny that this approach is appreciably more costly than alternatives. They further contend that dollars

---

[158] Avey, Markowitz and Reardon "Disentangling Grand Strategy," p. 40.
[159] Aaron L. Friedberg, *Beyond Air–Sea Battle: The Debate Over US Military Strategy in Asia* (London: Routledge, 2017).
[160] Montgomery, "Contested Primacy," p. 117.
[161] Brooks, Ikenberry and Wohlforth, "Don't Come Home America," p. 22.
[162] Nye, "East Asian Security," p. 95.
[163] Charles A. Kupchan and Peter L. Trubowitz, "Dead Center: The Demise of Liberal Internationalism in the United States," *International Security* 32, no. 2 (Fall, 2007): p. 43.

spent overseas to maintain American leadership benefits the American economy. Drezner characterizes these benefits as follows:

> One argument, which I label "geoeconomic favoritism," hypothesizes that the military hegemon will attract private capital because it provides the greatest security and safety to investors. A second argument posits that the benefits from military primacy flow from geopolitical favoritism: that sovereign states, in return for living under the security umbrella of the military superpower, voluntarily transfer resources to help subsidize the costs of hegemony. The third argument postulates that states are most likely to enjoy global public goods under a unipolar distribution of military power, accelerating global economic growth and reducing security tensions.[164]

Brooks and Wohlforth address the claim that deep engagement "imposes heavy costs and yields scant benefits," countering that it has produced broad national economic prosperity and security.[165] That view has been readily accepted in Washington for decades, often supplemented by a starker claim: that abandoning the liberal order will ultimately endanger American security.

Threats and Opportunities

Deep engagement prioritizes constraining great power adversaries, "as many great powers in the past have frequently done."[166] But proponents reject preventive great power war "driven by the perception of a rising adversary, the anticipation of a decline in relative power, and the fear of the consequences of decline"[167] because it is both illegal under international law and contrary to American strategic traditions.[168] Limiting the military tools for addressing challengers, the priority is to enmesh them within an institutional web of interdependence coupled with multilateral security institutions.

Deep engagement emphasizes varied threats to the status quo. "Deep Engagement Plus," for example, endorses humanitarian operations in the defense of human rights and stability, failed states therefore constituting a fertile ground for activity. The United States often commits itself to activism beyond a narrow conception of its national interests, the logic being that it can prevent localized conflicts from spreading into wider conflagrations that might threaten the liberal order. In practice, this may lead to "meeting threats when

---

[164] Drezner, "Military Primacy Doesn't Pay," p. 58.

[165] Ikenberry et al., "Don't Come Home," p. 15.

[166] Charles A. Kupchan and Peter L. Trubowitz, "Grand Strategy for a Divided America," *Foreign Affairs* 86, no. 71 (2007): p. 81.

[167] Jack S. Levy, "Preventive War: Concept and Propositions," *International Interactions* 37, no. 1 (2011): p. 87

[168] James J. Wirtz and James A. Russell, "U.S. Policy on Preventive War and Preemption, *The Nonproliferation Review* 10, no. 1, (2003): pp. 113–123.

and where they emerge,"[169] justified by the oft-reiterated claim that the United States is an "indispensable power."[170]

Optimistic proponents of deep engagement see significant global opportunities: spreading liberal democracy by enhancing the size and significance of a politically participatory and economically consumptive middle class; the institutionalization of the rule of law and human rights; and the expansion of global wealth to alleviate poverty. In effectively exporting American domestic values, the strategic goal is to enhance the United States' indispensable, benign hegemonic leadership.

3.2.3 Sponsorship

Definition and Scope

Sponsorship, the most recent innovation in grand strategy, has several distinct features. It eschews leadership, dominance or strategic non-engagement. It prioritizes solving global or regional collective action problems, embracing multilateralism without demanding the right to dominate or lead in agenda-setting, while still serving American national interests.[171] Sponsorship therefore requires strategic patience – awaiting rather than initiating agendas – which is at odds with America's traditional proactive, muscular political culture.[172]

Agendas promulgated by moral or norm entrepreneurs can result in formal laws, protocols and norms and be enshrined in global or regional governance institutions. These form the basis for actionable items. Alternatively, these items can be informally generated by a large group of countries and non-state actors.[173] In either case, others seek American assistance to address shared problems. These may include conventional national security concerns, such as the smuggling of fissile materials, but can extend to elements of human security such as global health, poverty, climate change and human rights.

A sponsorship grand strategy therefore adopts an expansive IR definition. In a complex global system, American national interests are best served when these match global collective initiatives. Under such circumstances, being viewed as a responsible global citizen enhances American legitimacy and leverage. The benefits that accrue from such engagement are immediate, such as greater burden sharing, but can potentially be broader because of the

---

[169] Montgomery, "Contested Primacy," p. 116.

[170] See, for example, "President Obama: What Makes Us America," *CBS*, September 28, 2014, www.cbsnews.com/news/president-obama-60-minutes/.

[171] Simon Reich, *Global Norms, American Sponsorship and the Emerging Patterns of World Politics* (Basingstoke and New York: Palgrave Macmillan, 2010), pp. 32–34.

[172] Simon Reich and Richard Ned Lebow, *Good-bye Hegemony!* p. 140.

[173] Reich and Dombrowski, *The End of Grand Strategy*.

goodwill generated. A sponsorship grand strategy thus entails the benefits of selective engagement without maldistributed material costs and accusations of American domination; and it can – in practice – avoid mission creep or inextricable entanglements.

Underlying Assumptions

Sponsorship strategies rest on four assumptions. First, that security is absolute, not relative. Safety is therefore not an excludable "club good."[174] This implies a positive-sum relationship, at least between collaborative actors, enhancing peace and cooperation and avoiding conflict except against clear adversaries.[175] Violence in a failed Central American state, for example, may threaten US security (through illicit drug, people and arms flows). If a demonstrably legitimate concern to national security, it justifies action under a sponsorship grand strategy.

Second, sponsorship is not altruistic. It serves the national interest. A precondition for engagement is therefore a consistency between national interests and those of the international community, including state, intergovernmental and nonstate actors. The logic has to be that sponsorship provides a tacit means for the United States to attain strategic goals that it either could not achieve unilaterally or where a unilateral approach would cost far more.

A third assumption addresses the importance of legitimacy. Sponsorship embraces the importance of the United States *being seen* to act as a responsible international stakeholder, rather than simply declaring itself one.[176] It relies on rational theories of collective action coupled with sociological theories of legitimation in IR.[177] Sponsorship focuses on implementation and enforcement to establish credibility. Operations may be coercive, but these have to be authorized by a consensual process in accord with the rule of law. In practice, the operational outcome sometimes replicates the effects of primacy or deep engagement: America playing the role of an indispensable power.[178] But the underlying justification for action differs between the exercise of unilateral, unauthorized power and of multilateral, authorized power. The

---

[174] Fen Osler Hampson, Jean Daudelin, John Hay et. al., *Madness in the Multitude: Human Security and World Disorder* (New York: Oxford University Press, 2002), pp. 39–40.

[175] Ibid., pp. 17–18.

[176] Steve Schiffres, "US Names Coalition of the Willing," *BBC*, March 18, 2003, http://news .bbc.co.uk/2/hi/americas/2862343.stm.

[177] Elinor Ostrom, "Collective Action and the Evolution of Social Norms," *Journal of Economic Perspectives* 14, no. 3 (Summer, 2000): pp. 137–158; Stacie E. Goddard and Ronald R. Krebs, "Rhetoric, Legitimation, and Grand Strategy," *Security Studies* 24, no. 1 (2015): pp. 5–36; Ian Clark, *Legitimacy in International Society* (New York: Oxford University Press, 2007).

[178] See, for example, Porter, 'Why America's Grand Strategy Has Not Changed," p. 9.

distinction is consequential.[179] The former signifies the capacity to act autonomously in defiance of others. Sponsorship, in contrast, signifies the authority to act in ways accepted by both the strong and the weak.[180]

Proponents of sponsorship construe international politics as a series of interlinked policies. A state may share immediate strategic interests that it cannot address unilaterally; but it also recognizes the advantages of building goodwill by acting in accordance with the interests of others so that it can enlist support when needed. Liberals often invoke NATO as an example of the institutional virtues of deep engagement. An advocate of sponsorship might respond differently, focusing on the legitimacy that the US had built up over decades as a provider of security: that its support for other countries was repaid by their adherence, after 9/11, to NATO's Article V (an attack on one member is an attack on all) – other NATO members agreed to participate in the military campaign in Afghanistan. Reciprocity through legitimacy thus looms large.

Geostrategic Objectives ("Ends")

A sponsorship grand strategy construes America's primary geopolitical interest as sustaining the international order. It therefore prioritizes stability by enforcing the rule of law and its associated norms, protocols and conventions while defying conceptions of the United States as a hyperpower.

Embedded in this formulation is the view that a dynamic global environment requires the United States to embrace sponsorship because the primary challenges it faces are only addressed by multilateral solutions. Terrorism, the proliferation of fissile materials, piracy, human trafficking, climate change and pandemics are just some of the examples where the US plays a critical role but is nonetheless reliant on a collaborative, coordinated response with both state and nonstate actors. Building walls – physical, technological, ideational or psychological – offers little protection in these cases.

The "Ways"

Sponsorship strategies entail a deliberative process. Agendas are often initiated by norm entrepreneurs advocating universal principles that uphold the rule of law or the protection of civilians, including possible humanitarian intervention.[181] Decisions are made through official, representative bodies that generate appeals

---

[179] Richard Ned Lebow and Simon Reich, "Influence and Hegemony: Shifting Patterns of Material and Social Power in World Politics," *All Azimuth* 6, no. 1 (January, 2017): pp. 17–48, www .foreignpolicyandpeace.org/wp-content/uploads/2016/09/ALL_AZIMUTH_Jan2017_WEB.pdf.

[180] This distinction is epitomized by the contrast between modern formulations of hegemony and ancient conceptions of *hégemonia*. Reich and Lebow, *Good-bye Hegemony!*, pp. 47–48.

[181] Reich and Lebow, *Good-bye Hegemony!*, pp. 148–149.

for American assistance.[182] This puts the United States in a powerful bargaining position. It inverts its customary position – from being depicted either as a bully or a supplicant – to being a benefactor, a sponsor, by shifting the onus of persuasion onto America's prospective partners. A consequence of that bargaining structure is that it helps avoid the propensity toward mission creep or open-ended commitments.[183] Three factors constrain this grand strategy: American action must be viewed as responsive, not proactive; it must be consistent with a collective interest; and it should address only behavior that is inconsistent with widely accepted international norms. Critically, policymakers do not preclude autonomous action when American national interests differ from those of other states. Sponsorship, in practice, allows policymakers to serve American interests in the context of a multilateral approach.

The Instruments ("Means")

Sponsorship uses the US military permissively, sometimes for constabulary purposes, like US operations to enforce the Proliferation Security Initiative against the smuggling of fissile materials.[184] These efforts are complemented by coercive diplomatic and legal initiatives. Since the George W. Bush administration, the US Department of State, for example, has effectively used the Trafficking in Persons (TIPS) Report, authorized by the Palermo Protocols and endorsed by numerous state and nonstate actors. TIPS Reports evaluate each country for possible trafficking offenses, with the threat of "naming and shaming" or economically sanctioning habitual transgressors.[185] Sponsorship therefore balances the use of instruments across different domains, judiciously employing diplomacy and lawfare (based on international law) as well as military instruments.

Threats and Opportunities

Sponsorship prioritizes global, flow-based threats to a rules-based system. Moisés Naim's "five wars of globalization"– drugs, arms trafficking, intellectual property theft, alien smuggling and money laundering – illustrate the problem.[186] Similarly, terrorism and piracy provide huge intelligence and enforcement challenges.[187] Proponents of sponsorship argue that, as failed American initiatives have repeatedly

---

[182] Reich, *Global Norms*, pp. 32–68.
[183] Reich and Lebow, *Good-bye Hegemony!*, pp. 147–154.
[184] Reich and Dombrowski, *The End of Grand Strategy*, chapters 5 and 6.
[185] See Reich, *Global Norms*, pp. 178–205.
[186] Naim, "The Five Wars of Globalization."
[187] Reich and Dombrowski, *The End of Grand Strategy*, pp. 85–121; Didier Bigo, "The Emergence of a Consensus: Global Terrorism, Global Insecurity and Global Security" in *Immigration, Integration and Security: America and Europe in Comparative Perspective*, eds. Ariane Chebel d'Appollonia and Simon Reich (Pittsburgh, PA: University of Pittsburgh, 2008) pp. 67–94.

demonstrated, neither unilateral action nor leadership strategies have contained these flows.[188] They maintain that they all require collective action and legal authorization to generate an effective response.[189] The same is true when battling naturogenic threats like pandemics, as a unilateral approach and criticism of international organizations has ably demonstrated in the case of COVID-19.[190] Addressing these problems requires relationships more reliant on cooperation and legal procedures, where the United States defers to local partners, albeit while providing valuable knowledge and materiel.[191]

Proponents maintain that addressing such threats helps consolidate the rule of law, a function central to sustaining the liberal world order. Ironically, the liberal order has come under increasing threat from the United States itself as a result of policy decisions made by the Trump administration that reduced US credibility: unilateral withdrawals from the Paris Agreement on climate change and the Joint Comprehensive Plan of Action, and abandonment of the embryonic Trans-Pacific Partnership Agreement. Still, the advantages of sponsorship may encourage future administrations to return to a sponsorship grand strategy.

3.2.4 Restraint

Definition and Scope

Restraint's paradox is that advocates want a large, powerful, globally capable military while seeking to limit the application of military force. The United States should have the capability to guard its preponderance in extremis – but to use it sparingly. This will both preserve its strength and leave sufficient resources for its domestic renewal. The scope of restraint is thus both simultaneously broad and constrained.

Proponents suggest that the United States should remain an open economy in a globalized system. It should "participate in international economic, environmental, and humanitarian agreements," support allies financially

---

[188] See Mark Aspinwall and Simon Reich, "Who Is Wile E. Coyote? Power, Influence and the War on Drugs," *International Politics* 53, (2016): pp. 155–175.

[189] Paul Miller, "How Does Jihadism End? Choosing between Forever War and Nation Building," *War on the Rocks*, September 11, 2016, https://warontherocks.com/2016/09/how-does-jihadism-end-choosing-between-forever-war-and-nation-building/.

[190] Laurel Wamsley, "Trump Criticizes WHO And Threatens To Pull U.S. Funding," *NPR*, April 7, 2020, www.npr.org/sections/coronavirus-live-updates/2020/04/07/829244345/trump-criticizes-who-and-threatens-to-pull-u-s-funding.

[191] The United States Armed Forces, *Joint Publication 3-22: Foreign Internal Defense* (Washington, DC: United States Armed Forces, 2010), www.jcs.mil/Portals/36/Documents/Doctrine/pubs/jp3_22.pdf. For African examples, see James Carden, "Why Are American Soldiers Fighting and Dying in Niger?," *The Nation*, October 24, 2017. www.thenation.com/article/why-are-american-soldiers-fighting-and-dying-in-niger/; Krishnadev Calamur, "The Region Where ISIS, Al-Qaeda, and Boko Haram Converge," *The Atlantic*, October 5, 2017, www.theatlantic.com/international/archive/2017/10/us-niger-green-berets/542190/.

when really necessary, and use sanctions robustly.[192] Global engagement would thus continue undiminished – with the exception of military responsibilities and entanglements. Restraint would return to President Thomas Jefferson's position, in his inaugural address, of "peace, commerce, and honest friendship with all nations, entangling alliances with none."[193] A "shaping" offshore global military presence, focused on key chokepoints in commanding the commons, "a strong military, just not a large or busy one," should reinforce those elements.[194]

Reducing profligate military spending, notably on American land forces, should be paramount. Yet, restraint, employing a classical definition of grand strategy, remains firmly focused on militarized instruments. Domestic economic renewal's central purpose is to provide a means to ensure that America's military, particularly its sea services and air force, can prevail in war. As Posen states, "A grand strategy is a nation-state's theory about how to produce security for itself. Grand strategy focuses on military threats, because these are the most dangerous, and military remedies because these are the most costly."[195] Eugene Gholz, Daryl Press and Harvey Sapolsky endorse that view, linking security to prosperity but ultimately, as Realists, they argue that, "Of America's goals, the highest priority is the physical security of the United States – the protection of territory and the ability to make domestic political decisions as free as possible from foreign coercion."[196] Furthermore, "economic strength is the foundation for long-term security, because wealth can be converted into military power."[197]

Assumptions

Nonetheless, advocates of restraint believe that the United States is fundamentally safe: they "tend to believe that the United States is quite secure, due to its great power, its weak and agreeable neighbors, and its vast distance from most of the world's trouble, distances patrolled by the U.S. Navy."[198] Significantly, it possesses a large and diverse set of nuclear weapons and delivery systems. Even its most capable nuclear peers, Russia and China, can at best maintain a relationship of mutual deterrence.

---

[192] Eugene Gholz, Daryl G. Press, and Harvey M. Sapolsky "Come Home, America: The Strategy of Restraint in the Face of Temptation," *International Security* 21, no. 4 (Spring, 1997): p.30.

[193] Thomas Jefferson, "First Inaugural Address," March 4, 1801, available online at the Avalon Project at Yale Law School (unpaginated), https://avalon.law.yale.edu/19th_century/jefinau1.asp.

[194] Ibid., p. 6.

[195] Posen, *Restraint*, p. 1.

[196] Gholz, Press and Sapolsky, "Come Home, America," p. 8.

[197] Ibid., p. 9.

[198] Barry R. Posen, "Stability and Change in U.S. Grand Strategy," *Orbis* 51, no 4 (Fall, 2007): p. 565.

The underlying logic of restraint is driven by two theories: balance of power theory, based on a historic conception of Britain as a seafaring balancer, and imperial overstretch – that the United States is overcommitted and declining relative to its great power competitors.[199] While not an unqualified advocate of restraint, Christopher Layne attributes US decline to two major factors: first, "the emergence of new great powers in world politics and the unprecedented shift in the center of global economic power from the Euro-Atlantic area to Asia" and, second, "the relative – and in some ways absolute – decline in America's economic power."[200] The activism of primacy and deep engagement will accelerate decline by frittering away American resources to reassure and defend relatively wealthy allies ("cheap-riders"), or being dragged into conflicts by allies on issues beyond core US national interests ("reckless drivers").[201] Drezner, however, questions the assumption that military preponderance itself is sufficient: "Military supremacy on its own is insufficient to prevent the renewal of great power tensions in the world; full-spectrum unipolarity is necessary. Without a sufficient amount of economic power, the pacifying effects of military supremacy will eventually erode."[202]

Geostrategic Objectives ("Ends")

The United States should specifically "refocus its efforts on its three biggest security challenges: preventing a powerful rival from upending the global balance of power, fighting terrorists, and limiting nuclear proliferation."[203] Of these, Posen argues that terrorism is the least critical because terrorists do not threaten America's "sovereignty, territorial integrity or power position."[204] Nuclear nonproliferation matters most because limiting regional powers' access to nuclear weapons reduces the probability that the United States might have to fight a nuclear-armed adversary in the future.[205] Proponents tend to be sanguine, believing that the great and growing powers in the Eurasian landmass – China, Russia, and India – face significant obstacles to becoming worthy rivals.

---

[199] Paul K. MacDonald and Joseph M. Parent, "Graceful Decline? The Surprising Success of Great Power Retrenchment," *International Security* 35, no. 4 (Spring, 2011): pp. 7–44.

[200] Christopher Layne, "This Time It's Real: The End of Unipolarity and the 'Pax Americana'," *International Studies Quarterly* 56, no. 1 (March, 2012): p. 204.

[201] Posen, *Restraint*, pp. 35–44.

[202] Drezner, "Military Primacy Doesn't Pay," p. 77.

[203] Barry R. Posen, "Pull Back: The Case of a Less Activist Foreign Policy," *Foreign Affairs* 92, no. 116 (January/February, 2013): p. 123.

[204] Ibid., p. 124.

[205] Ibid., p. 125. Other proponents of restraint view nuclear proliferation differently: "an activist security policy does not reduce the danger," partially because it will increase the likelihood that the United States will become a nuclear target; Gholz, Press and Sapolsky, "Come Home, America," p. 39.

The "Ways"

The objective is to attain a balanced force structure that will allow the United States to decisively project power. A restraint grand strategy "requires a powerful, full-spectrum, and deployable military that invests heavily in technology and uses realistic training to improve capabilities and deter challenges. Restraint demands a military with a global reach that is sparingly used."[206] That force structure would allow "a significant reduction in the number of active-duty forces and a significant reduction in America's overseas military presence."[207] Proponents assert that defense spending could fall as much as 50 percent.[208]

Posen asserts that "U.S. security guarantees also encourage plucky allies to challenge more powerful states, confident that Washington will save them in the end – a classic case of moral hazard." They thus incur "political costs, antagonizing powers great and small for no gain and encouraging them to seek opportunities to provoke the United States in return."[209] Restraint therefore eschews military alliances, preferring "ad hoc coalitions, friendly diplomatic engagement, trade agreements, cultural exchanges, and other means."[210] The United States should reduce its commitment to NATO and the Persian Gulf region because European allies can defend themselves in the former and national interests are insufficient in the latter.[211]

The Instruments ("Means")

Posen reflects a clear consensus regarding appropriate grand strategic instruments. America's military should prioritize command of the global commons underpinning US preponderance: a unilateral reliance on air, sea and space forces that denies potential or current adversaries the ability to undermine American interests.[212] The objective is to retain a decisive position in global balancing. But the military should not be forward deployed. Its power can largely be exercised from the US homeland (by long-range missiles, the air force and space capabilities).

The United States would maintain sufficient sea and air forces "to protect the ability to use the sea lanes to assist allies, in order to protect regional balances of power."[213] Naval forces should also dominate the open oceans. The army would

---

[206] Harvey M. Sapolsky, Benjamin H. Friedman, Eugene Gholz and Daryl G. Press, "Restraining Order: For Strategic Modesty," *World Affairs* 172, no. 2 (Fall, 2009), p. 86.

[207] Gholz, Press and Sapolsky, "Come Home, America," p. 14.

[208] Sapolsky et al., "Restraining Order," p. 65.

[209] Posen, "Pull Back," p. 122.

[210] Sapolsky et al., "Restraining Order," p. 87.

[211] Gholz, Press and Sapolsky, "Come Home, America," pp. 17–29.

[212] Barry R. Posen, "Command of the Commons: The Military Foundation of U.S. Hegemony," *International Security* 28, no. 1 (Summer, 2003): pp. 5–46.

[213] Posen, "Stability and Change," p. 566.

be reduced with personnel and bases pared.[214] Heavily armed, combat-capable land forces would be limited, reserved largely for the unlikely event that any great power should threaten to dominate the Eurasian landmass or challenge US control of the commons.

Economic, social and cultural engagement should be left to private interests. But advocates abhor the idea of exporting American values or institutions. Activities associated with promoting democracy or neoliberal economic policies abroad would be insignificant under a grand strategy of restraint.

Threats and Opportunities

Gholz, Press and Sapolsky are explicit: Command of the commons is essential. Intervention is only acceptable if another great power "develop[s] the conventional capabilities for rapid conquest of its neighbors"; "threaten[s] to bring together enough power after its conquests to either mount an attack across the oceans or threaten U.S. prosperity by denying America access to the global economy"; or if the United States needs to "overcome the nuclear capabilities of other great powers."[215] But – unlike a large swath of the national security establishment – they believe these possibilities are unlikely. America should thus focus on global chokepoints, albeit a position complicated by China's efforts to assert sovereignty over the commercially invaluable South China Sea.[216] Although focused on threats, opportunities are defined strategically by the capacity to enhance command of the commons, predominantly through technological innovation in defense capabilities rather than military intervention.

3.2.5 Isolationism

Definition and Scope

For Bear Braumoeller, isolationism "is best thought of as the voluntary and general abstention by a state from security-related activity in an area of the international system in which it is capable of acting."[217] Eric Nordlinger likewise characterizes isolationism as a process of "strategic non-engagement."[218] This grand strategy is idiosyncratic because a survey of the historical literature reveals

---

[214] Posen, *Restraint*, pp. 159–160.

[215] Gholz, Press and Sapolsky "Come Home, America," pp. 46–47.

[216] Center for Strategic and International Studies, "How Much Trade Transits the South China Sea?," China Power Project (undated), https://chinapower.csis.org/much-trade-transits-south-china-sea/#easy-footnote-bottom-1-3073.

[217] Bear F. Braumoeller, "The Myth of American Isolationism," *Foreign Policy Analysis* 6 (2010): pp. 349–371 (354).

[218] Eric Nordlinger, *Isolationism Reconfigured: American Foreign Policy for a New Century* (Princeton, NJ: Princeton University Press, 1995), p. 3.

that it is often associated with nativism and racism. Its conceptual basis as a grand strategy, however, stems from its analytic distinction between security-related policies and those in the economic or political spheres: Commercially, the United States has rarely abstained from global markets.

Politically, isolationism was not inevitably linked to ethnic or racial exclusion before the 1930s. Presidents, from Washington to Wilson, in distinguishing the United States from the nasty politics of Europe, argued that: "Americans deprecate power politics and old-fashioned diplomacy, mistrust powerful standing armies and entangling peacetime commitments, make moralistic judgments about other people's domestic systems, and believe that liberal values transfer readily to foreign affairs."[219] Interwar isolationists subsequently favored this perspective.

Underlying Assumptions

Stephen Walt identifies isolationism's key assumptions as follows: "[T]he United States has few security interests beyond its borders, . . . threats to these interests are modest, and . . . very limited means (a small army, a coastal navy, and a modest nuclear deterrent) are sufficient to protect them."[220] Walter Russell Mead characterizes this sentiment as part of a Jacksonian tradition.[221] All scholars of isolationism emphasize strategically chosen inaction, at least beyond the Western Hemisphere.

Additionally, isolationism relies on several other assumptions. First, that sovereignty and territoriality are indistinguishable and sacrosanct, and thus the extraterritorial application of power is rarely, if ever, desirable. Second, that America –surrounded by three great oceans (the Atlantic, Pacific and the Arctic) and two militarily weak neighbors – has little need for a large, expensive military. Third, that a variety of contemporary legal and illicit flows – of drugs, guns, money and even people – can be deterred or regulated by the state. Border security can create an effective barrier. The Trump administration's focus on undermining the registration process for asylum-seekers arriving through Mexico, on constructing a massive southern wall or in instituting a ban on Muslims arriving from certain countries personified this belief.

---

[219] Joseph Lepgold and Timothy McKeown, "Is American Foreign Policy Exceptional? An Empirical Analysis," *Political Science Quarterly* 110, no.3 (Autumn, 1995): p. 369. This view has persisted. See "Outrage at 'Old Europe,' Remarks," *BBC News*, January 23, 2003, http://news.bbc.co.uk/2/hi/europe/2687403.stm.

[220] Stephen M. Walt, "The Case for Finite Containment: Analyzing U.S. Grand Strategy," *International Security* 14, no.1 (Summer, 1989): p. 7.

[221] Walter Russell Mead, "The Jacksonian Revolt: American Populism and the Liberal Order," *Foreign Affairs*, March/April, 2017, www.foreignaffairs.com/articles/united-states/2017-01-20/jacksonian-revolt.

Finally, and perhaps most controversially, there is the assumption that "more contact equals more friction," at least when it comes to security policy. Christopher Preble broadly endorses this sentiment when arguing that reducing America's military power will paradoxically make it more secure: Having too large a military encourages policymakers to use it; reducing capacity will reduce the temptation.[222] Preble emphasizes that he is not an isolationist, describing its historically nativist sentiments as "odious."[223] But advocates of isolationism embrace this assumption. Seen through this optic, Jihadism is a "blowback" product of American foreign policy – a view expressed by isolationists on the political Left, if not the Right.[224]

Committed Isolationists – like former congressman Ron Paul – are rare.[225] Nonetheless, many politicians espouse policies consistent with isolationism, which is often driven by electoral calculations and party-political commitments. As Robert Urbatsch concludes, "domestic partisan politics drives a considerable fraction of the putative public support for isolationist policy ... to the extent that mass opinion affects governmental foreign policy choices—unpopular governments will face greater constraints in prosecuting international agendas since the public will tend to resist foreign engagements."[226] As opinion polls occasionally demonstrate, isolationism is popular, albeit combined with a preference for a large military.[227]

Geostrategic Objectives ("Ends")

The main geostrategic debate among isolationists is how far beyond the nation's territorial borders its security perimeter should extend. One fundamentalist version addresses this question in even narrower terms – of building actual walls that insulate American territory from illicit flows with maritime perimeters confined to the American littoral.[228] Eric Nordlinger advocates an "exceptionally narrow security perimeter ... around North America," claiming that "Other than protecting the international sea- and air-lanes to and from the

---

[222] Christopher Preble, *The Power Problem* (Ithaca, NY: Cornell University Press, 2009), p. 3.

[223] Ibid., p. 10.

[224] Chalmers Johnson, *Blowback: The Costs and Consequences of American Empire* (New York: Metropolitan Books, 2010).

[225] Ron Paul, *Liberty Redefined: 50 Essential Issues That Affect Our Freedom* (New York: Hachette Book Group, 2011).

[226] Robert Urbatsch, "Isolationism and Domestic Politics," *Journal of Conflict Resolution* 54 no. 3, (2010): pp. 487–488.

[227] Bruce Stokes, "American Isolationism, with a Very, Very Big Stick," Pew Research Center, May 17, 2016, www.pewresearch.org/global/2016/05/17/american-isolationism-with-a-very-very-big-stick/.

[228] See Reich and Dombrowski, *The End of Grand Strategy*, chapter 8.

water's edge, the strategy demands a true minimum of security-centered involvements beyond North America."[229]

A third position redefines America's geographic span as a sphere of influence – dating back to the Monroe Doctrine of 1823. Although largely aspirational, it sought to exclude European powers from operating in the Western Hemisphere. Robert Tucker, invoking Walter Lippmann's views expressed in the midst of World War II, concurs that isolationists share a "conviction that the nation's security was unconditioned by events occurring beyond the Western Hemisphere."[230]

Contemporary isolationists are committed to withdrawing from security alliances and relationships but recognize the need for regional engagement. Many are concerned with China's growing activities in Latin America and support interdicting illicit flows at a distance, in practice the Caribbean, Mexico and Central America's Northern Triangle.[231] But intervention often extends further South into countries like Colombia, from which cocaine exports to the United States originate.[232]

The "Ways"

Paradoxically, given the preference for disengagement, some isolationists assume that the United States should globally serve as "a moral example."[233] While this sentiment waxed from John Winthrop's "City on the Hill" sermon aboard the Arabella in 1630 to the isolationist position of the 1930s, it still remains an element today. It has often expressed itself through a white nativism directed against cultural and racial aliens, political radicals or criminals,[234] the Republic being a superior form of governance.

Yet nativism and an isolationist grand strategy are not synonymous. Indeed, a progressivist version rails against modern forms of American imperialism, suggesting that retrenchment would serve as a panacea for a slew of budgetary and security problems.[235] Libertarians concur, focusing on domestic renewal

[229] Nordlinger, *Isolationism Reconfigured*, p. 3.
[230] Robert W. Tucker, *A New Isolationism: Threat or Promise?* (New York: Universe Books, 1972), p. 40.
[231] Amelia Cheatham, "Central America's Turbulent Northern Triangle," Council on Foreign Relations, October 1, 2019, www.cfr.org/backgrounder/central-americas-turbulent-northern-triangle.
[232] Christopher Woody, "Here's How Drugs Are Getting Smuggled from South America to the US," *Business Insider*, September 14, 2017, www.businessinsider.com/heres-how-drugs-are-getting-smuggled-from-south-america-to-the-us-2017-9.
[233] Tucker, *A New Isolationism*, p. 30.
[234] Julia G. Young, "Making America 1920 Again? Nativism and US Immigration, Past and Present," *Journal on Migration and Human Security* 5, no. 1, 2017: pp. 217–235, https://doi.org/10.1177/233150241700500111.
[235] Johnson, *Blowback*, pp. 19–20.

as a means of arresting "overreach." Both concur in abstaining from military competition, favoring diplomatic and private sector commercial engagement.

The Instruments ("Means")

Isolationists, predictable given the controversial label "America Firsters," are unilateralists.[236] They favor autonomy. It is a common misnomer, however, to assume that isolationism entails pacifism, reduced defense spending or even smaller military forces. Historically, isolationists have taken comfort in America's vast oceans and its weak neighbors.

Yet, simultaneously, while technological innovation and globalization may have diminished geography's influence on security, nuclear weapons and missile systems have strengthened the isolationist logic. Their abundance and the United States' mutually assured destruction (MAD) relationship with the Soviet Union (and then Russia) has helped create a "Fortress America" that protects the American homeland from conventional, territorial threats.[237] Noted Realist, Stephen Krasner, has even suggested that: "Nuclear weapons have made the world a much more stable place, and this stability would be enhanced by a policy of neo-isolationism."[238] And, of course, the United States has long invested in the US Coast Guard for coastal defense.[239] The creation of the Department of Homeland Security, and its proposed budgetary growth to over $70 billion in 2020, has only served to reinforce the *national* in the term "national defense."[240]

Threats and Opportunities

Shorn of major national security concerns, isolationists have tended to prioritize hemispheric flows of people and contraband (weapons, at one time whisky and eventually drugs) that they believe internally weaken the United States. Yet, such flows were and remain a product of domestic demand and enterprising smugglers. Americans have been complicit with weak or corrupt foreign governments that seek to raise revenue and are unable to enforce treaties or

---

[236] Robert W. Tucker, "Isolation & Intervention," *The National Interest*, no. 1 (Fall, 1985), p. 17.

[237] "Remove that theme [the defense of freedom], and the only reason for any army at all is to prevent a landing on the beaches of Miami. And for that a coast guard and a few thousand nuclear warheads will do nicely"; Charles Krauthammer and Malcolm Fraser, "Isolationism: A Riposte," *The National Interest*, no. 2 (Winter, 1985/6): p. 118.

[238] Stephen D. Krasner, "Realist Praxis: Neo-Isolationism and Structural Change," *Journal of International Affairs* 43, no. 1 (Summer/Fall, 1989): p. 159.

[239] Reich and Dombrowski, *The End of Grand Strategy*, pp. 142–160.

[240] US Department of Homeland Security, "Budget-in-Brief: Fiscal Year 2020," p. 1, www.dhs.gov /sites/default/files/publications/19_0318_MGMT_FY-2020-Budget-In-Brief.pdf.

domestic laws.[241] More recently, terrorism and the potential for smuggling weapons of mass destruction and resulting large casualties have raised the profile of territorial security. Yet even the most committed isolationists recognize the importance of cooperation with source countries (for example, intelligence sharing) and the establishment of long-distance security procedures and capabilities (such as at foreign airports) to prevent illicit flows. This militates against pure unilateralism, but is nonetheless a regrettable concession for what Didier Bigo labels "the classics" seeking insulation.[242]

3.3 Conclusion

We have presented five different ideal types, in an attempt to answer fundamental questions. Sometimes the responses overlap, yet the result is five unique configurations, represented in Table 2 on page 49.

Beyond the individual elements, what clearly stands out is their comparative variance in terms of their conception of the purpose of grand strategy. The answer to that question helps define other elements that follow, including each type's relative reliance on instruments in each domain. Table 3 on page 50 supplements Table 2 by comparing the relative forms and the balance of instruments adopted by each approach.

There is a clear distinction that can be drawn between types of grand strategies when the two tables are combined. Doing so allows for certain kinds of comparison. Certainly, it allows for a systematic comparison of different American grand strategies over time – the substance of the next section.

Of course, it is questionable whether these types can be readily used to analyze other states. Global primacy is not an option for any other state (except, potentially, China), although regional primacy is an option entertained by a few. Versions of a liberal or sponsorship strategy are arguably pursued by numerous states (large and small), while isolationism was widespread (under the guise of autarky) in the Soviet Bloc during the Cold War and remains in a few outposts today. Thus, while not fitting for all states, this set of types has a comparative utility as a benchmark for adjudging the features of other states, both historically and in the contemporary realm. Furthermore, the conceptual underpinnings of other states' grand strategies often resemble those found in the United States. As we demonstrate in section 5, where we compare the interactions of states within the Indo-Pacific, strategic parallels appear with India and China. The rationale underpinning, for example, India's long-standing principal of

---

[241] Peter Andreas, *Smuggler Nation: How Illicit Trade Made America* (London: Oxford University Press, 2014).

[242] Didier Bigo, "The Emergence of a Consensus," pp. 84–86.

Table 2 Five types of grand strategy

	Primacy	Deep engagement	Sponsorship	Restraint	Isolationism
Definition	Classical	IR	IR	Classical	Classical
Primary actors	States	States, Corporations, International organizations, Transnational criminal organizations	States, IOs, norm entrepreneurs, NGOs, TCOs, Corporations	States	States, TCOs, terrorists and migrants
Relationship	Zero-sum	Positive-Sum	Positive-Sum	Zero-sum	Zero Sum
Operating principle	Domination	Leadership, first among equals	Equal before the law/norm	Offshore balancing	Strategic nonengagement
Mode of behavior	Unilateral	Multilateral	Adjuvant	Selectively unilateral	Unilateral
Underlying theory	Power transition Offensive Realism	Hegemonic stability	Legitimation theory	Balance of power	Defensive Realism
Geostrategic objectives ("ends")	Sustain hierarchical international order	Maintain institutionalized liberal order	Enforce international norms and law for stability	Command the commons	Control border or hemispheric flows
"Ways"	Large-scale militarization and economic sanctions	Balanced use of institutionalized economic, diplomatic and military instruments	Diplomacy and lawfare backed by economic and military policing of global flows	Moderated militarization within a restructured force capacity	Nuclear capacity, homeland security and diplomatic engagement
"Means"	Demographics, industrial capacity, size of economy Political capacity	Forward platforms Alliance structures Burden sharing Institution building Aid, trade and finance	Global interdiction Technological intelligence and communications capacity Burden sharing	Control of air, sea, space chokepoints through nuclear and air force navy and space force	Nuclear forces, Coast guard and border control Diplomacy and trade agreements
Definition of threats	Narrow – national security Primary focus on conventional threats on land and sea	Broad – attacks on global institution and nation building, and on economic interdependence	Broadest – international, and national security with a focus on illicit or naturogenic flows	Narrow – threats to power position through loss of authority over chokepoints	Very narrow –illicit flows undermining domestic sovereignty, or territorial integrity
Definition of opportunities	Narrow – geostrategic natural resource or tactical advantage	Broad – promotion of rule of law, capitalism, technological innovation or possibly human rights	Broad – building legitimacy for cooptation in addressing collective action problems	Narrow – maximizing national interest with minimal engagement and cost	Very narrow – sustaining domestic resources for economic renewal

Table 3 The domains and instruments of grand strategy

Primacy	Deep engagement	Sponsorship	Restraint	Isolation
Military force (coercive)	Military force (coercive and US-led)	Military force (Military operations other than war and rotational command)	Military force (navy, space, air force)	Military force (navy, air force, US Coast Guard, national guards, law enforcement agencies)
Diplomacy (nominal)	Diplomacy (moderate)	Diplomacy (moderate to high)	Diplomacy (low to moderate)	Diplomacy (low)
Institution building (national)	Institution building (global)	Institution building (global and regional)	Institution maintenance (global and regional)	Institution maintenance (global and regional)
Lawfare (low)	Lawfare (moderate to high)	Lawfare (high)	Lawfare (low)	Lawfare (low)

nonalignment bear elements of some versions of American isolationism. With Xi's emergence, China's grand strategy certainly suggests regional primacy with global pretensions.

In section 4, however, we compare how the first three American presidents of the twenty-first century have applied distinct grand strategies in Europe.

4. Comparing Administrations over Time: Continuity and Change

Our discussion until this point in outlining the possible forms of grand strategy has been largely conceptual. But ideal types never match the complicated reality of actual planning, strategy, policy and operations. These are invariably overwhelmed by contingency, chance and subject to the vagaries of domestic politics. Scholars often label a presidential administration with one kind of grand strategy: The Reagan administration, for example, reputedly pursued an especially expansive variant of containment against the Soviet Union.[243] In

---

[243] Barry R. Posen and Stephen Van Evera, "Defense Policy and the Reagan Administration: Departure from Containment," *International Security* 8, no. 1 (Summer, 1983): pp. 3–45; Fareed Zakaria, "The Reagan Strategy of Containment," *Political Science Quarterly* 105, no. 3 (Autumn, 1990): pp. 373–395.

reality, as we have shown, presidents simultaneously run multiple versions of the ideal types we describe.[244] They perennially mix and match, with a preference for specific formulations in a particular theater of conflict or for specific issue areas. In general, presidents often predominantly favor an awkward combination, driven by threats and occasionally by opportunities.

Our goal in this section is to illustrate how comparisons can be made over time. We do so across three successive American administrations spanning two decades. Comparing successive administrations (as cases) in this way allows us to hold as many factors constant as possible – the historical, cultural, political and institutional – when trying to identify the key sources of change. Here, we examine the predominant approaches of George W. Bush, Barack Obama and Donald Trump in a historically important region for the United States (Europe) and in relation to a particular adversary (Russia).[245]

Of course, leadership changes, as do circumstances. But we purposively chose three presidents that served in the post 9/11 period because it is widely regarded as a watershed in American foreign relations, especially in regard to Europe. Furthermore, in the aftermath of 9/11, there were three common, identifiable trends: (1) NATO, and Europe more generally, joined the US campaign to defeat al-Qaeda, Iraq and then the Islamic State in the Global War on Terror; (2) Russia reemerged and grew as a major military threat; and (3) Europe increasingly came under pressure from the flows of refugees both by land and by sea.[246] Yet successive US administrations significantly varied their behavior toward Russia as these trends only nominally evolved.

Indeed, the United States has only been consistent in its inconsistency. This cannot be explained by systemic factors of the type emphasized by Realists. Rather, harkening back to our claims in section 2, it is due to the changing nature of American domestic politics, both institutionally and ideologically. The former has been reflected in the gradual erosion of relations between the Chief Executive and his staff, Department of Defense, military services and various intelligence agencies, culminating in the fragmentary impetus of the Trump administration. The latter has been marked in the increasing polarization of politics and policy. In defiance of former Chairman of the Senate Foreign Relations Committee Arthur Vandenberg's famous adage, politics no longer

---

[244] Reich and Dombrowski, *The End of Grand Strategy*. See also Colin Dueck, "Hybrid Strategies: The American Experience," *Orbis* 55, no. 1 (2011): pp. 30–52.

[245] This choice contrasts nicely with the emergent theater we examine in the next section (the Indo-Pacific) and the major states – including China – we discuss.

[246] Peter Dombrowski and Simon Reich, "The EU's Maritime Operations and the Future of European Security: Learning from Operations Atalanta and Sophia," *Comparative European Politics* 17 (2019): pp. 860–88 4.

"stops at the water's edge." In tandem, these domestic factors have made it extremely difficult to maintain strategic consistency across administrations.[247]

In the three mini–case studies that follow, we briefly discuss each administration's relationship with European states and the differing means of coping with the challenges posed by Russian behavior. Unlike Trump, Bush and Obama (in differing ways) maintained their support for NATO and, after Obama's initial effort at a reset, a distrust of Russia. Yet each mixed elements of standard grand strategies. Bush often combined the Liberal ends of nation building with primacist military instruments, producing a neoconservative elixir. Obama often sought Liberal ends and ways (democracy promotion and multilateralism) but increasingly favored military restraint (emphasizing burden sharing and reduced military commitments), punctuated by direct military strikes (often using armed drones) against America's enemies.[248] Finally, Trump combined isolationist ways (military retrenchment and greater burden sharing) with operationally primacist ends (combatting great power competition).

4.1 The Bush Administration and Benign Neglect

George W. Bush, as candidate and then as President until 9/11, was not especially interested in or broadly knowledgeable about foreign affairs, despite the tutoring of Condoleezza Rice and a host of experts who became known as the "Vulcans."[249] Yet Bush was "very much determined to do things differently from his predecessor."[250] On the campaign trail, for example, Bush "derided the Clinton administration for appeasing a rising China and indulging a corrupt Russia."[251] The conventional view was that his administration was besotted with American power and believed that any rising challenger had to be confronted and repressed.[252]

---

[247] Charles A. Kupchan and Peter L. Trubowitz, "Dead Center: The Demise of Liberal Internationalism in the United States," *International Security* 32, no. 2 (Fall, 2007): pp. 7–44. For a subsequent debate, see Joseph M. Parent, Joseph Bafumi, Charles A. Kupchan and Peter L. Trubowitz, "Correspondence: Of Polarity and Polarization," *International Security* 33, no. 1 (Summer, 2008), pp. 170–173. For a later view, see Charles A. Kupchan and Peter L. Trubowitz "American Statecraft in an Era of Domestic Polarisation" in *After Liberalism? The Future of Liberalism in International Relations*, eds. Rebekka Friedman, Kevork Oskanian and Ramon Pacheco Pardo (New York and Basingstoke, UK: Palgrave, 2013), pp. 117–144.

[248] Trevor McCrisken, "Obama's Drone War," *Survival* 55, no. 2 (2013): pp. 97–122.

[249] Notably Richard Armitage, Robert Blackwill, Stephen Hadley, Richard Perle, Paul Wolfowitz, and Dov Zakheim as discussed in James Mann, *Rise of the Vulcans: The History of Bush's War Cabinet* (New York: Penguin Books, 2004).

[250] Ivo H. Daalder and I. M. Destler, "In the Shadow of the Oval Office: The Next National Security Adviser," *Foreign Affairs* 88, no. 1 (January/February, 2009): pp. 114–129.

[251] James M. Lindsey, "George W. Bush, Barack Obama and the Future of US Global Leadership," *International Affairs* 87, no. 4 (2011): p. 768.

[252] See Draft of FY 94-99 Defense Planning Guidance (DPG), in Dale A. Vesser to Secretaries of Military Departments, Chairman of the Joint Chief of Staff et al., February 18, 1992, Electronic Briefing Book (EBB) 245, National Security Archive (NSA).

As President, Bush drew upon several foreign and defense experts who had served in his father's administration: Donald Rumsfeld in his second term as Secretary of Defense; Colin Powell as Secretary of Defense; and Condoleezza Rice as National Security Advisor.[253] None were considered ideologues; indeed, most could be termed "Conservative Internationalists" who largely adhered to a Cold War set of precepts.[254] Only a few second-tier officials, such as Undersecretary of Defense Paul Wolfowitz, had any acknowledged neoconservative credentials.

4.1.1 The 9/11 U-turn and Europe's Estrangement

The 9/11 attacks changed everything. They highlighted Bush's inexperience,[255] depleted the influence of the Republican "wise men" who had served in his father's administration, and undermined the precepts on which Bush had campaigned. While the source of this change is contested, Ivo Daalder and Mac Destler plausibly argue that Rice proactively decided to "channel Bush – to focus on his instincts and translate them into policy."[256] Thus, rather than push the mainstream Republican views that had prevailed in George H. W. Bush's administration, she helped unleash George W.'s policy preferences, no matter how ill-informed. Thus, bolstered by domestic unanimity among politicians and the public in support of military action (first in Afghanistan and then in Iraq), the administration seized on a more aggressive, primacist approach that focused on regime change and, when necessary, unilateral action. While the war against the Taliban generated both initial sympathy and acquiescence among American allies,[257] the subsequent objective of regime change in Iraq spawned widespread mistrust abroad.[258]

---

[253] As befitting a member of the Vulcans, Condoleezza Rice set the tone for those who would join the new administration. She stressed the importance of great powers Russia and China, but feared Russia's weakness rather than its strength. The proliferation of Russian nuclear materials, technology and expertise was her main concern. Regarding Europe, Rice recommended strengthening NATO. Condoleezza Rice, "Campaign 2000: Promoting the National Interest," *Foreign Affairs* 79, no. 1 (January/February, 2000): pp. 45–62.

[254] On "conservative internationalism," see Henry R. Nau, *Conservative Internationalism: Armed Diplomacy under Jefferson, Polk, Truman, and Reagan* (Princeton, NJ: Princeton University Press, 2015); Paul D. Miller, *American Power and Liberal Order: A Conservative Internationalist Grand Strategy* (Washington, DC: Georgetown University Press, reprint edition, 2018), pp. 110–112.

[255] "After meeting the Russian in Slovenia in June 2001, Bush legendarily exclaimed that he had caught a glimpse of Putin's 'soul' "; Samuel Charap and Timothy J Colton, "Cold Peace," in "Everyone Loses: The Ukraine Crisis and the Ruinous Contest for Post-Soviet Eurasia," *Adelphi Series* 56, no. 460 (2016): pp. 17–28.

[256] Daalder and Destler, "In the Shadow of the Oval Office," pp. 125–126.

[257] Philip H. Gordon, "NATO after 11 September," *Survival* 43, no. 4 (2001): pp. 89–106.

[258] Michael MacDonald, *Overreach: Delusions of Regime Change in Iraq* (Cambridge, MA: Harvard University Press 2014).

This controversial decision proved of lasting consequence, altering US relations with Europe and, in many ways, shaping the Bush administration's ability to respond to Russian aggression in the President's second term. While the Bush administration formally consulted with the UN and key allies, it was clear early on that the United States would not take no for an answer. Key administration officials were viewed as deceptive.[259] Consultations, even with the United Kingdom, were often pro forma and helped pit leaders like Prime Minister Tony Blair against parts of his own government.[260] As more intelligence emerged following the invasion of Iraq, American credibility with many European allies was seriously damaged.

After the initial support for NATO's mission in Afghanistan (the International Security Assistance Force or ISAF),[261] many European partners tired of the war and increasingly restricted their contributary forces' operations.[262] More significantly, European allies volubly questioned the justification for and conduct of the endless war in Iraq. Its contentious origins, and the struggle to maintain control against a raging insurgency, provided significant obstacles to morale and cohesion.[263] Further aggravating both war efforts was tension over the neoconservative objectives of US grand strategy, with its focus on regime change using military power to both punish aggressors and create a more democratic world.[264] Operationally, NATO's de facto raison d'etre had incrementally shifted, from the defense of Europe to regime change elsewhere. In the words of American diplomat Nicholas Burns we "now find that our entire agenda is pivoting from an inward focus on Europe to an outward focus ... U.S.-European relations are increasingly a function of events in the Middle East, Asia and Africa."[265] To this could be added maritime operations from the Mediterranean and off the Horn of Africa.[266] As NATO enlarged – ten states

---

[259] Walter LaFeber, "The Rise and Fall of Colin Powell and the Powell Doctrine," *Political Science Quarterly* 124, no. 1 (Spring, 2009); pp. 71–93, especially p. 89.

[260] David T. Owen, "Good Faith and (Dis)Honest Mistakes? Learning from Britain's Iraq War Inquiry," *Politics* 37, 4 (2017) pp. 371–385.

[261] Initially the Bush administration rejected NATO involvement in Afghanistan because "the deployment of forces to Iraq left the United States needing more help in securing and rebuilding Afghanistan"; Ivo Daalder and James Goldgeier, "Global NATO," *Foreign Affairs* 85, no. 5 (September/October, 2006), p. 108.

[262] David P. Auerswald and Stephen M. Saideman, *NATO in Afghanistan: Fighting Together, Fighting Alone* (Princeton, NJ: Princeton University Press 2014).

[263] Philip Gordon and Jeremy Shapiro, *Allies at War: America, Europe and the Crisis Over Iraq* (New York: McGraw-Hill 2004).

[264] Jonathan Monten, "The Roots of the Bush Doctrine: Power, Nationalism, and Democracy Promotion in U.S. Strategy," *International Security* 29, no. 4 (Spring, 2005): pp. 112–156.

[265] Quoted in Daalder and Goldgeier, "Global NATO," p. 109.

[266] See, for example, Reich and Dombrowski, *The End of Grand Strategy*, pp. 85–102.

were admitted in 2004 – membership was tied to both democratization and combatting the Global War on Terror.[267]

By the beginning of Bush's second term, it was clear that the relative neglect of European concerns had allowed a number of contentious issues to fester.[268] Allies objected to his administration's policies, notably with regard to the Israeli–Palestinian conflict, tactics in the war on terror, missile defense strategy and climate change. Above all, there was the neglected issue of the humiliation of Russia and defense of Europe.

4.1.2 Diplomatic Fiasco

This realization of allies' concerns was amplified early in Bush's second term, when he and senior members of his foreign and defense team made several trips to European capitals in an effort to mend fences. Cognizant of the growing problem, newly appointed Secretary of State Condoleezza Rice declared, in August 2008, "the time for diplomacy is now."[269] First, she publicly recognized European contributions, especially in NATO's "out-of-area" operations. Then, noting a diplomatic triumph for the United States of benefit to Europe, Rice touted the administration's new "strategic framework" agreement, signed with Russia.[270]

Rice's timing could not have been worse. Russia immediately invaded Abkhazia and South Ossetia in Georgia under the pretext of "peace enforcement" operations (to supposedly protect Russian minorities). Even Bush's sympathizers admitted that his administration erred during this period: initially in provoking Russia by openly discussing Georgian and Ukrainian membership of NATO, and then by failing to adequately respond in the aftermath of the Russia incursions.[271]

Georgia was an important test of the Bush administration's commitment to Europe. After encouraging the Georgia government to apply for NATO membership and pushing other NATO members to consider membership for states in the Caucasus, the Bush administration backed down when Russia (inevitably, some

---

[267] Andrew T. Wolff, "The Future of NATO Enlargement after the Ukraine Crisis," *International Affairs* 91, no. 5 (2015): p. 110 8.

[268] Wolff calls this period a "temporary abatement of tension in the early 2000s"; Wolff, "The Future of NATO Enlargement," pp. 1108–1109.

[269] Philip H. Gordon, "The End of the Bush Revolution," *Foreign Affairs* 85, no. 4 (July/August, 2006): p. 81.

[270] Condoleezza Rice, "Rethinking the National Interest: American Realism for a New World," *Foreign Affairs* 87, no. 4 (July/August 2008): pp. 16–26.

[271] Hal Brands and Peter Feaver, "The Case for Bush Revisionism: Reevaluating the Legacy of America's 43rd President," *Journal of Strategic Studies* 41, no. 1-2 (2018): p. 2, https://doi.org /10.1080/01402390.2017.1348944.

argue) reacted with military force. It helped ship Georgian troops deployed in Iraq back home and promised to rebuild the postwar Georgian military. But the administration provided little or no other direct military support to Georgia, refusing to even impose economic sanctions on Russia or withdraw from the Sochi Olympics. Angela Merkel "summed up the majority view in the EU when she refused to put all the blame for the war on Russia's shoulders, but acknowledged that 'some of Russia's actions were not proportionate'."[272] Merkel's attitude, and US inaction, left frontline states in eastern Europe increasingly wary of Russia and uncertain about American commitment to their defense – an issue that would reverberate over the next decade.

The Bush administration's relations with Europe, both in Europe itself and in "out-of-area" operations, were caught between soaring rhetoric and political realities. While calling for NATO expansion and support for democratic governments on the eastern frontier with Russia, the administration simultaneously demanded European support in Afghanistan and, to a lesser extent, Iraq. Further, the administration's freedom to maneuver diplomatically was limited by the changing domestic political landscape. Iraq had proved problematic, no weapons of mass destruction had been found, and it was increasingly clear to the American public that the US military was bogged down in counterinsurgency operations. Meanwhile, in Afghanistan, the Taliban has largely recovered from its early defeat in 2001–2.

The post-9/11 turn of the Bush administration towards a neoconservative focus on democratization, regime change and aggressive efforts to confront the challengers – big and small – to American primacy called for a level of effort on the part of the American people that they were not willing to bear for very long. Foreign policy critics at home and abroad warned against imperial overstretch and rising antagonism to the United States, and expressed concern that other countries might imitate American policies.[273] Adventurism also conflicted with the domestic focus of the Bush policy agenda. As Melvyn Leffler observed, "The ends of Bush's foreign policy cannot be reconciled with domestic priorities that call for lower taxes."[274]

Those two decisions, to encourage NATO membership and then not react following Russia's invasion, arguably altered indelibly the path of US–Russia relations, from a position of American dominance in the 1990s to sustained

---

[272] Mike Bowke, "The War in Georgia and the Western Response," *Central Asian Survey* 30, no. 2 (2011): p. 198.

[273] Colin Dueck, "Hegemony on the Cheap: Liberal Internationalism from Wilson to Bush," *World Policy Journal* 20, no. 4 (Winter, 2003/2004), p. 8.

[274] Melvyn P. Leffler, "Think Again: Bush's Foreign Policy," *Foreign Policy*, October 23, 2009, https://foreignpolicy.com/2009/10/23/think-again-bushs-foreign-policy/.

conflict after 2008. Russia has subsequently remained an abiding source of contestation between the United States and its European allies. Certainly, by the time Bush left office, his misleading of the public over the reasons for invading Iraq had polarized the electorate, divided the national security community and alienated European allies.[275] Departing from a strategy designed to extend NATO's community of nations up to Russia's border, his successor, Barack Obama, would attempt to heal the rupture with both Russia and European leaders as one of his major foreign policy initiatives during his first term, while retreating from grandiose overseas military commitments. President Obama's own policy preferences, the fiscal constraints of the Great Recession and the preferences of his own electoral base would ensure the new administration would retreat from the ambitions of its predecessor.

4.2 Barack Obama, Europe, the Reset and the Pivot

Barack Obama also came to office without a strong background in international affairs.[276] He too, however, had an experienced foreign and security policy team to rely on – many having served in prior Democratic administrations. Yet the biggest single guiding factor shaping Obama's grand strategy was a financial and economic crisis that was soon labeled "the Great Recession." As a consequence, the President prioritized ways to stabilize both the US and global economies. Indeed, cognizant of their economic and political costs, his administration sought to wind down two costly "forever wars" and tamp down growing problems with Russia. Both issues were central to US relations with European governments and NATO itself: first, because many European contributors to ISAF were looking to withdraw and, second, because few European states were then interested in confronting Russia.

Under the circumstances, Obama's grand strategy predominantly combined elements of two ideal types: restraint and sponsorship, which Dan Drezner has characterized as counterpunching.[277] The former was "designed to curtail the United States' overseas commitments, restore its standing in the world, and shift burdens onto global partners."[278] In Libya and Syria, the latter was condemned by critics as "leading from behind."[279] Among those critics, Colin Dueck

---

[275] Robert Legvold, *Return to Cold War* (Cambridge, UK: Polity 2016).

[276] In fairness to the last seven presidents, only Geoge H. W. Bush can be said to have had deep knowledge and experience in international affairs.

[277] Daniel W. Drezner, "Does Obama Have a Grand Strategy? Why We Need Doctrines in Uncertain Times," *Foreign Affairs* 90, no. 4 (July/August, 2011), p. 58.

[278] Ibid.

[279] Charles Krauthammer, "The Obama Doctrine: Leading from Behind," *Washington Post*, April 28, 2011, www.washingtonpost.com/opinions/the-obama-doctrine-leading-from-behind /2011/04/28/AFBCy18E_story.html.

characterized Obama's grand strategy as "overarching American retrenchment and accommodation."[280]

Unlike Bush's reliance on instinct, David Axelrod characterized this President as "no drama Obama" – reflective, deliberative and risk averse.[281] As noted in a famous 2016 interview, "Obama would say privately that the first task of an American president in the post-Bush international arena was 'Don't do stupid shit'."[282] Restraint (reducing commitments and enhancing diplomacy) and sponsorship (avoiding mission creep) were expressions of that rationale in a way that was palatable for many voters. It was far less palatable for what has come to be known as "the Blob" foreign policy professionals who, according to Francis Gavin's summary of Stephen Walt's position, "have a vested interest in seeing the United States pursue liberal hegemony, even as the strategy has failed, because it creates work and opportunities for them."[283]

4.2.1 Russia and the Reset

After the Bush administration's hubris, and relative neglect of Russia and Europe, Obama entered office with a reconciliatory agenda. In the administration's first major foreign policy speech at the Munich Conference on Security in February 2009, Vice President Biden promised to "press the reset button" on relations with Russia and reassured American allies and partners that "We'll engage. We'll listen. We'll consult."[284] This approach appeared to achieve tangible short-term objectives including, "greater logistical access to northern entry points into Afghanistan to support the NATO war effort there, cooperation in sanctioning Iran and North Korea, as well as the conclusion of a New START Treaty in 2010."[285] Critics abounded, of course, but largely on suspicion that the approach was not sustainable, and that a host of traditional American policy

---

[280] Colin Dueck, *The Obama Doctrine: American Grand Strategy Today* (New York: Oxford University Press 2015), p. 2.

[281] Ed Rogers, "The Insiders: The Problem with 'No-Drama Obama'," *Washington Post*, January 13, 2014, www.washingtonpost.com/blogs/post-partisan/wp/2014/01/13/the-insiders-the-problem-with-no-drama-obama/.

[282] Jeffrey Goldberg, "The Obama Doctrine," *The Atlantic*, April, 2016, www.theatlantic.com/magazine/archive/2016/04/the-obama-doctrine/471525/.

[283] Francis J. Gavin, "Blame It on the Blob? How to Evaluate American Grand Strategy," *War on the Rocks* (August 21, 2020), https://warontherocks.com/2020/08/blame-it-on-the-blob-how-to-evaluate-american-grand-strategy/ – review of Stephen M. Walt, *The Hell of Good Intentions: America's Foreign Policy Elite and the Decline of U.S. Primacy* (New York: Farrar, Straus and Giroux, 2018)

[284] James Blitz, "Biden Proposes to 'Press Reset Button' with Moscow in Munich," *Financial Times*, February 7, 2009, www.ft.com/content/21cb9768-f525-11dd-9e2e-0000779fd2ac.

[285] Clifford Gaddy and Michael O'Hanlon, "Toward a 'Reaganov' Russia: Russian Security Policy after Putin," *The Washington Quarterly* 38, no. 2 (2015): pp. 206–207.

preferences with regard to Russia – such as human rights and democratization – had been sacrificed.[286]

But efforts at restoring equilibrium in US–Russia relations and reembedding these in a wider European security architecture soon began to falter, largely because of an incapacity to institutionalize trust and cooperation over hard security issues. This culminated in 2014 with Russia's dramatic incursions into Crimea and eastern Ukraine.[287] Why Putin annexed Crimea and began a hybrid conflict in eastern Ukraine is debatable, but most explanations place much weight on Putin's need to defend greater Russia against Western incursion, sustain Russia's historical imperialism or even satisfy his own gambler's instincts.[288] Few explanations predominantly blame Obama's efforts at resetting US–Russia relations.

4.2.2 Europe and the Pivot

Europe had been the focal point during the Cold War and a reliable if rambunctious partner during the first two decades of the post–Cold War era. Bush had moved that focus to the Middle East. By early 2011, senior American officials began to signal a comparable major foreign and security policy shift. Secretary of State Hillary Clinton pronounced it "America's Pacific Century."[289] Whether intended or not,[290] this signaled to many Europeans that their continent had again been downgraded in American grand strategy. Europe would have to rely more on its own resources in facing a resurgent Russia and the various challenges on the southern tier. By some accounts, it represented an opportunity for Europe to develop an independent grand strategy.[291] Meanwhile, the United States would shift attention and resources to the Pacific, because of both China's growing military capacity in the Indo-Pacific and Asia's increasing centrality to global commerce.

---

[286] Ruth Deyermond, "Assessing the Reset: Successes and Failures in the Obama Administration's Russia policy, 2009–2012," *European Security* 22, no. 4 (2013): pp. 500–523, especially pp. 504–507.

[287] Jeffrey Mankoff, "The Tricky U.S.-Russia 'Reset' Button," Council on Foreign Relations, February 17, 2009, www.cfr.org/expert-brief/tricky-us-russia-reset-button.

[288] Céline Marangé, "Russian Grand Strategy" in Balzacq, Dombrowski and Reich, *Comparative Grand Strategy*, pp. 50–72; Daniel Treisman, "Why Putin Took Crimea: The Gambler in the Kremlin," *Foreign Affairs* 95, no. 3 (May/June, 2016): pp. 47–54.

[289] Hillary Clinton, "America's Pacific Century," *Foreign Policy* 89 (November, 2011): pp. 56–63.

[290] Ibid., p. 63. It didn't help that Clinton omitted mentioning Europe until she tepidly relegated the continent to "traditional allies" and "partners of the first resort," in contrast to the many paragraphs extolling America's Asian friends and allies.

[291] Doug Stokes and Richard G. Whitman, "Transatlantic Triage? European and UK 'Grand Strategy' After the US Rebalance to Asia," *International Affairs* 89, no. 5 (2013): pp. 1087–1107.

In contrast to Bush's cajoling of European allies in Iraq, the Obama administration was therefore reluctantly prepared to sponsor a European initiative in Libya, providing munitions, intelligence and transport in support of mostly French and British forces.[292] Subsequently, the Russian annexation of Crimea forced an ongoing campaign in Eastern Ukraine and compelled the Obama administration to redeploy forces, first as a United States only European Reassurance Initiative (ERI) and later as NATO's European Deterrent Initiative (EDI). The ERI, announced in June 2014, was a $1 billion initiative (for one year) to reassure allies, especially in Eastern Europe, of continued US commitment to their security in the face of Russia's latest aggression. Funded from the Department of Defense's fiscal year 2015 Overseas Contingency Operations budget (the same budget that funds the war in Afghanistan and other operations in the Middle East), the ERI provided largely symbolic forward deployments of small numbers of land forces, increased maritime patrols in the Black Sea, and organized more Air Force training and exercises.[293] After this modest initial response, the United States strengthened its position and enhanced its activities until 2017. The operation was then renamed the EDI. The EDI continues to this day despite President Trump's professed antipathy to NATO. EDI funds – roughly $5 billion for fiscal year 2020 – largely support "the presence of additional rotational U.S. forces in Europe" as well as the prepositioning of equipment, improved infrastructure, and increased training.[294]

In sum, when the Russia reset failed to stabilize US–Russian relations and perhaps allow for reduced American contributions to European defense, the Obama administration committed funding and forces to shore up NATO's frontline defenses and help deter Russia from further armed aggression. President Obama's response was firmly embedded within NATO – a long-standing multilateral institution – at the 2016 Warsaw Summit that established "Enhanced Forward Presence" (EFP) to include committing four battalion-sized units to be deployed to Estonia, Latvia, Lithuania and Poland under UK, Canadian, German and US leadership.[295] On the other hand, the long-term issue of American responsibility to its European partners and allies remained, and

---

[292] Reich and Lebow, *Good-bye Hegemony!*, pp. 142–154.

[293] Office of the Press Secretary, "FACT SHEET: European Reassurance Initiative and Other U.S. Efforts in Support of NATO Allies and Partners," The White House, June 3, 2014, https://obamawhitehouse.archives.gov/the-press-office/2014/06/03/fact-sheet-european-reassurance-initiative-and-other-us-efforts-support-.

[294] US European Command Public Affairs Office, "FY 2020 European Deterrence Initiative (EDI) Fact Sheet."

[295] Mark Zapfe, "Deterrence from the Ground Up: Understanding NATO's Enhanced Forward Presence," *Survival* 59, no. 3 (2017): pp. 147–160.

reemerged stronger than ever when President Trump took office in January 2017.

4.3 Donald Trump: Personality, Populism and America First

Donald Trump was entirely inexperienced in international affairs and any form of governing, having never served in elected office. Similarly, the President's advisors overwhelmingly lacked any international experience. Foreign and security policy experts who analyzed his campaign statements, looking for a coherent underlying philosophy, found none. Early assessments of a possible grand strategy ranged from a new variant of isolationism,[296] to Jacksonian population[297] or illiberal hegemony which, according to Barry Posen, seeks to maintain US economic and military superiority while forsaking democracy promotion and multilateral free trade.[298]

In contrast, some authors, for example, Mark Beeson, suggested that Trump took a transactional approach: "Trump believes that his personal qualities, especially in combination with America's economic importance and strategic might, will allow him to negotiate bilateral deals that have eluded other presidents, especially Obama."[299] A second set even debated whether President Trump and his administration could even have a grand strategy,[300] while a third argued that Washington's national security policy establishment, labeled the "Blob," ensured that Trump's grand strategy would default to approximating that of his predecessors.[301]

Yet it may be that these formulations missed the essential feature of Trump's approach to grand strategy. His administration labeled it "principled Realism" in the *National Security Strategy* (*NSS*, 2017) and the *National Defense Strategy* (*NDS*, 2018), which prioritized "protect[ing] the American people, the homeland, and the American way of life; ... promot[ing] American prosperity ... preserv[ing] peace through strength ... advanc[ing] American influence."[302] Principled Realism, to many, sounded like an oxymoron given its supposed confluence between narrow self-interest and American values. And so it proved. The public record, and observed behavior, suggest that the national security

---

[296] Rubrick Biegon, "A Populist Grand Strategy? Trump and the Framing of American Decline," *International Relations* 33, no.4 (2019): pp. 517–539.

[297] Taesuh Cha, "The Return of Jacksonianism: The International Implications of the Trump Phenomenon," *The Washington Quarterly* 39, no. 4 (2016): pp. 83–97.

[298] Barry R. Posen, "The Rise of Illiberal Hegemony: Trump's Surprising Grand Strategy," *Foreign Affairs* 97, no. 2 (March/April, 2018): pp. 20–27.

[299] Mark Beeson, "Donald Trump and Post-Pivot Asia: The Implications of a 'Transactional' Approach to Foreign Policy," *Asian Studies Review* 44, no. 1 (2020): p. 11.

[300] Peter Dombrowski and Simon Reich, "Does Donald Trump Have a Grand Strategy?," *International Affairs* 93, no. 5 (2017): pp. 1013–1037.

[301] Porter, "Why America's Grand Strategy Has Not Changed," pp. 9–46.

[302] *The National Security Strategy of the United States of America*, December, 2017.

community indeed settled on a confluence between two elements. But both were based on narrow self-interest. First, there was a primacist approach in the Departments of Defense and State that sought primarily to prevent other great powers from destabilizing the American-led international system or coercing the United States to leave key geopolitical regions like the South China and the Baltic Seas.[303] Second, an isolationist element emerged in Homeland Security, tinged with nativism, entailing a focus on border control to subjugate flows of migrants, drugs, pandemics and commerce.

4.3.1 Europe's Continued Neglect?

It is routinely claimed that the Trump administration clearly did not prioritize Europe relative to other regions; at best, it can be seen as a region where the United States pursued offshore balancing.[304] The problem with this assessment is that it runs square up against both Trump's *NSS* and *NDS* which prioritized great power competition, particularly with Russia and China. The *NSS* clearly stated that: "Russia seeks to restore its great power status and establish spheres of influence near its borders."[305] Given that Russia borders NATO forces, this posed a clear challenge for American grand strategy. With a frozen conflict in Ukraine, ongoing saber-rattling in the Baltics and Arctic, and aggressive military behaviors against American and allied forces in Europe, Russia poses the main regional threat to peace and security.

Conversely, political ambiguity hung over Trump's own attitude toward Russia, and consequently the American commitment to Europe. Trump criticized European allies and praised Putin. Yet major strategic documents focused on Russia: The US military trains and exercises alongside other NATO members to defend against Russia and an Enhanced Forward Presence sent a clear signal of America's willingness to deter and defend against Russian regional aggression.[306]

In effect, the administration pursued an ambivalent approach to Russia. The President and his closest associates carefully avoided confrontation over Russian transgressions in Europe, the greater Middle East, the Indo-Pacific or even inside the United States itself. Trump spoke effusively in defense of Russia

---

[303] Ashley Townsend, Brendan Thomas-Noone and Matilda Steward, "Averting Crisis: American Strategy, Military Spending and Collective Defence in the Indo-Pacific," United States Study Center, August 19, 2019, www.ussc.edu.au/analysis/averting-crisis-american-strategy-military-spending-and-collective-defence-in-the-indo-pacific.

[304] James McKay, "How Transatlantic Is the Trump Administration?" *Journal of Transatlantic Studies* 17, (2019): pp. 532–553.

[305] *The National Security Strategy of the United States of America*, December, 2017, p. 25.

[306] Martin Zapfe, "Deterrence from the Ground Up: Understanding NATO's Enhanced Forward Presence," *Survival* 59, no.3 (2017): pp. 147–160.

in the course of Congressional investigations, although these comments were self-serving, tied to his own legitimacy in being elected president in 2016. Conversely, the bureaucracies under his command – especially the Department of Defense, the military services, the combatant commands and agencies of the intelligence community – competed dangerously with Russia. *The NDS* summarized their view of the challenge:

> Concurrently, Russia seeks veto authority over nations on its periphery in terms of their governmental, economic, and diplomatic decisions, to shatter the North Atlantic Treaty Organization and change European and Middle East security and economic structures to its favor. The use of emerging technologies to discredit and subvert democratic processes in Georgia, Crimea, and eastern Ukraine is concern enough, but when coupled with its expanding and modernizing nuclear arsenal the challenge is clear.[307]

The *NDS* pledged to "Fortify the Trans-Atlantic NATO Alliance" to meet this challenge. Yet it reiterated that: "We expect European allies to fulfill their commitments to increase defense and modernization spending to bolster the alliance in the face of our shared security concerns."[308] Correspondingly, Trump repeatedly broke protocol in public, aggressively berating other NATO leaders over their failure to increase defense spending and expressing a willingness to consider withdrawing from NATO. He did this even at sensitive times, such as when meeting to discuss potential Ukraine and Georgia NATO accession in 2019.[309]

However, Trump's behavior and the *NDS* reflect a schism between the Chief Executive, the bureaucracy and, eventually, a previously demure congressional leadership. Congress worked legislatively to prevent the President from taking unilateral action over NATO membership,[310] and both the Department of Defense and the intelligence community continued apace with programs to solidify Europe's defense and deter Russia. Resistance within the US national

---

[307] Jim Mattis, *Summary of the 2018 National Defense Strategy: Sharpening the American Military's Competitive Edge* (Washington, DC: The White House 2018), p. 2 (a classified version has not been released). https://dod.defense.gov/Portals/1/Documents/pubs/2018-National-Defense-Strategy-Summary.pdf.

[308] Ibid., p. 9.

[309] Julian E. Barnes and Helene Cooper, "Trump Discussed Pulling U.S. from NATO, Aides Say Amid New Concerns over Russia," *New York Times*, January 14, 2019, www.nytimes.com /2019/01/14/us/politics/nato-president-trump.html. Bush and Obama had encouraged greater burden sharing, but in a more measured way; Christina Wilkie, "Trump Is Pushing NATO Allies to Spend More on Defense. But So Did Obama and Bush," *CNBC*, July 11, 2018, www.cnbc.com/2018/07/11/obama-and-bush-also-pressed-nato-allies-to-spend-more-on-defense.html.

[310] Joe Gould, "Would Trump Drive NATO Exit? Congress Works on Roadblocks," *Defense News*, December 16, 2019, www.defensenews.com/congress/2019/12/16/would-trump-drive-nato-exit-congress-works-on-roadblocks/.

security community to the further weakening of NATO suffered a severe blow when President Trump and Secretary of Defense Mark T. Esper reportedly announced the number of American troops stationed in Germany would be capped at 25,000 – a 9,500 reduction.

Significantly, the EDI continued unabated, backed by strong congressional support, with the United States continuing to spend roughly $5 billion per year and providing for significant rotational deployment of US army, navy and air forces in the Baltics and the Black Sea region – the regions thought most vulnerable to further Russian mischief. The conundrum of America's willingness to underwrite NATO remains unresolved, yet is perhaps a bit closer to reform.

4.4 A Point in Time

This section can only point to a few highlights when comparing three administrations' strategies toward European allies and adversaries. But even this cursory examination shows that there have clearly been three different approaches. External threats and opportunities slowly changed – principally, growing Russian aggression. But that cannot explain the dramatic difference between the Bush administration's cavalier neoconservatism and diplomatic naivete, the Obama administration's hesitant sponsorship of European interventions and discarding of its Russian reset and the Trump administration's mystifying criticism of allies, coupled with the paradoxical rhetorical deference and yet operational primacist containment strategy toward Russia. Each was based on different assumptions, resulting in a difference of ends, ways and means. Bush assumed that the United States could cow Russia by surrounding it using NATO forces and by promoting democracy. Obama sought to repair the transatlantic diplomatic rift that had developed, initially, at least, with Russia and continually with Europe. He then reassured allies and consolidated the US contribution to NATO deterrence when Russia behaved aggressively in Ukraine and then in Syria. Trump, on the other hand, relied less on traditional coalition building and reassurance. But he generally allowed the US military and intelligence communities to prioritize Russia as a threat and took steps, with NATO, to maintain American military primacy. Trump greatly amplified burden sharing as an issue, but that had been an underlying theme for both the Bush and Obama administrations.

Two key factors are unknown at the time of writing. The first is if Joe Biden's victory in the 2020 presidential election will ease the fractures that have found their way into both the national security establishment and the electorate's polarization. A second is how American allies and friends will respond to Biden's overtures for greater transatlantic cooperation. A Trump victory would certainly have presaged tension, troop withdrawal and greater urgency for Europe to develop greater "strategic autonomy" as its leaders tired of Trump's behavior but feared Russian aggression.[311] Less certain is a European response to a Biden administration's desire for rapprochement and restorative effort to reassert multilateral leadership. Biden's victory may have come as a relief to many in Europe. But that may not be enough to abate domestic demands for a greater independent European capacity.

In this section we have examined three proximate administrations in one key region to demonstrate their enormous variance. Surprisingly, little changed in two decades, yet the elements of American grand strategy altered considerably. More space would allow us to examine those elements more rigorously and in greater detail, working through the sources and consequences of change. But the lesson to be drawn is that systematic comparison is possible and the domestic sources discernible if a framework is followed.

5. Grand Strategies in the Indo-Pacific

Our primary goal in this section is to provide an illustration of how grand strategies can be interactive, competitive and comparable: how grand strategies intersect, conflict and reinforce each other. We chose the recently reframed Indo-Pacific region because it is the globe's locus of economic dynamism.[312] It is also widely regarded as a more likely venue for a major war. One option is that North Korea will attack South Korea and/or fight the United States. Other potentially dangerous conflicts could occur between the region's nuclear powers, for example, India with China or Pakistan. Indo–Sino border skirmishes prompt fears of an escalation, as do worries that Kashmir will provoke a Pakistan–India war. Most prominently, there are fears that China and the United States are now embroiled in a Thucydides

---

[311] Alexandra Brzozowski, "In Munich, Macron Presents EU Reform As Answer to 'Weakening West'," *Euroactiv*, February 15, 2020, www.euractiv.com/section/future-eu/news/in-munich-macron-presents-eu-reform-as-answer-to-weakening-west/; Josep Borrell, "The Pandemic Should Increase Our Appetite to Be More Autonomous," European Union External Action, July 4, 2020, https://eeas.europa.eu/headquarters/headquarters-homepage/82060/pandemic-should-increase-our-appetite-be-more-autonomous_en; Richard Higgott and Simon Reich, "Hedging by Default: The Limits of EU 'Strategic Autonomy' in a Binary World Order," LSE IDEAS, (undated) https://www.lse.ac.uk/ideas/publications/reports/hedging-by-default.

[312] Andre Gunder Frank, *ReORIENT: Global Economy in the Asian Age* (Berkeley and Los Angeles: University of California Press 1998).

Trap in which a declining hegemon and rising challenger fight – with global implications.[313]

We focus on China, India and the United States. We fully recognize that only examining these three states does scant justice to the complex regional dynamics and does not pay sufficient attention to the importance of other major actors – from Australia, Indonesia, Japan and South Korea among the large states, to the city-state of Singapore that sits at a pivotal geographic point. But given the inevitable tension between depth and breadth, we have chosen depth. The section is also limited in that it will examine the enduring and evolving dimensions of state strategies since 9/11. That event may not have been critical for China and India, on which we primarily focus. But it critically changed American strategizing, the largest external actor in the region, and therefore interactively influenced its behavior.

5.1 China and the Indo-Pacific

From the end of the Cold War until 2015, the dominant position in Washington and Europe's capitals was that China's rhetoric of a peaceful rise accurately reflected its grand strategy – a modernizing nation focused on internal economic development and greater global integration[314] that would evolve into a "responsible stakeholder."[315] Doing so would require that China "make both absolute and relative gains in both its material and its status positions ... without precipitating major hostilities between itself and either its neighbors or other major powers."[316] Accomplishing this feat would entail a "strategic reassurance to China's neighbors and major powers that China's ascension will not threaten their economic or security interests."[317] Zheng Bijan, a major Chinese theorist, expressed this sentiment in rejecting the central notion of power transition that rising powers inevitably challenge the global order and provoke conflicts with dominant status quo powers.[318]

Many observers, however, sensed a change in China's overarching grand strategy with President Xi Jinping's assumption of power in 2014. Rather than

---

[313] Graham Allison, *Destined for War: Can America and China Escape Thucydides' Trap?* (New York: Mariner Books, 2018).

[314] Zheng Bijan, "China's Peaceful Rise to Great-Power Status," *Foreign Affairs* 84, no. 5 (September/October, 2005): pp. 18–24.

[315] Amitai Etzioni, "Is China a Responsible Stakeholder," *International Affairs* 83, no. 3 (2011): pp. 539–553.

[316] Barry Buzan, "China in International Society: Is 'Peaceful Rise' Possible?," *The Chinese Journal of International Politics* 3, (2010): p. 5.

[317] Bonnie S. Glaser and Evan S. Medeiros, "The Changing Ecology of Foreign Policy-Making in China: The Ascension and Demise of the Theory of 'Peaceful Rise'," *China Quarterly* 190, (June, 2007): pp. 291–310.

[318] Ibid., pp. 291–310.

"peaceful rise 2.0,"[319] critics charged that it was becoming increasingly aggressive – economically and militarily, regionally and globally. Xi has subsequently reshaped China's approach to the point where there is widespread concern that it does indeed have expansive objectives.[320] New economic and diplomatic relations appeared to be designed to ensure that China can maintain access to natural resources for supplies, global markets for exports and even reshape regional and international institutions to give it more influence in multilateral fora. It has created institutional alternatives including the Shanghai Cooperation Organization and the Asian Infrastructure Investment Bank.[321] Concurrently, it has systematically modernized its armed forces,[322] notably the People's Liberation Army Navy (PLAN) – the armed service most useful in projecting military power globally – as it vigorously reasserted its claims and capacities in the East and South China Seas.

5.1.1 Xi and China's Dream

China's leaders and foreign policy commentariat have adopted a more assertive approach to its external relations, some recently linked to domestic political developments associated with the "China Dream." This narrative focuses on a "great national rejuvenation," defined as a "prosperous, strong, and harmonious" country – to be achieved by 2049, the centenary of the Chinese Communist Party's (CCP) ascent to power. As Michael Clarke has commented: "Although the 'China Dream' has often been understood as a domestically oriented strategy to embed the legitimacy of the CCP, it also has clear foreign policy dimensions. Achieving 'great national rejuvenation' will not only consolidate CCP rule domestically, but also provide Beijing with the capability to 'preserve' a peaceful external environment."[323] China's actions have matched this rhetorical shift, best exemplified by elements in two domains: The Belt and Road Initiative (BRI) economically and the tremendous growth in the capabilities and ambitions of the PLAN militarily. They have become a source of concern for

---

[319] Jian Zhang, "China's New Foreign Policy under Xi Jinping: Towards 'Peaceful Rise 2.0'?" *Global Change, Peace & Security* 27, no. 1 (2015): pp. 5 –19.

[320] Andrew S. Erickson, "China," in Balzacq, Dombrowski and Reich, *Comparative Grand Strategy*, pp. 73–98.

[321] Chien Peng Chung, "China and the Institutionalization of the Shanghai Cooperation Organization," *Problems of Post-Communism* 53, no. 5 (2006): pp. 3–14; Hong Yu, "Motivation behind China's 'One Belt, One Road' Initiatives and Establishment of the Asian Infrastructure Investment Bank," *Journal of Contemporary China* 261, no. 05 (2017): pp. 353–368.

[322] M. Taylor Fravel, *Active Defense: China's Military Strategy since 1949* (Princeton, NJ: Princeton University Press, 2019).

[323] Michael Clarke, "The Belt and Road Initiative: Exploring Beijing's Motivations and Challenges for Its New Silk Road," *Strategic Analysis* 42, no. 2 (2018): p. 86.

China's neighbors as well as India and the United States, the Indo-Pacific's two other pivotal powers.

5.1.2 The Belt and Road Initiative

Xi's policies have fulfilled the desire for global economic integration expressed in the "peaceful rise" theory. China's internal growth has been matched by its massive exports and overseas investments. But the strategic Achilles' heel of the Chinese domestic economy is its dependence on maritime transport for exporting goods and importing the natural resources necessary for sustaining its industrial growth and emerging consumer economy. Initial efforts to secure sea lines of communication by building a "string of pearls" from the Chinese littoral to the Eastern Mediterranean soon confronted the "Malacca Dilemma." As Hu Jintao stated in 2003, the problem stems from the geographic reality that the most efficient route for shipping to flow between the West and China has to pass through the strategic chokepoint of the Malacca Strait where they might be vulnerable to wartime interdiction.[324] The BRI is designed to free China from the maritime Malacca Dilemma by focusing "on greater economic interconnectivity through the improvement of critical infrastructure such as oil and gas pipelines, highways, railways and telecommunications networks gels with the long-held desire of Central Asia's energy rich states to diversify export routes for their oil and gas and need for infrastructure investment."[325]

Debates rage on BRI's role within China's grand strategy, ranging from BRI as a top-down initiative aimed at leveraging its economic power to alter the Western-built international order, to a more organic, fragmented process driven by a myriad of Chinese economic stakeholders.[326] This debate is inconsequential for the United States, India and those countries affected by China's BRI investment patterns. Regardless of its intent, BRI disrupts local economies, alters domestic politics and increases the economic, political and security vulnerabilities of participating states. It therefore represents a strategic challenge to India and the United States.

5.1.3 Red Star Rising: The PLAN

The BRI can be connected to the quickening ascent of the PLAN to the premier ranks of the world's navies. As Zhengyu Wu contends: "China's latest shift in

---

[324] Marc Lanteigne, "China's Maritime Security and the 'Malacca Dilemma'," *Asian Security* 4, no. 2 (2008): pp. 143–161.

[325] Michael Clarke, "The Neglected Eurasian Dimension of the 'Indo-Pacific'," *Security Challenges* 16, no. 3 (2020): p. 36.

[326] Michael Clarke, "The Belt and Road Initiative," *Asia Policy* 24, (July, 2017): pp. 71–79.

naval strategy [toward a 'blue water' navy capable of influencing the open seas] is a logical corollary of the tension between its globally expanding national interests and peculiar asymmetric approach to sea power, while the newly unveiled BRI provides the necessary stimulus and justification for such a shift."[327]

The growth of the PLAN has been remarkable. It is not necessarily unprecedented in the size and number of ships and other warfighting platforms. But it is likely unique in the pace of the accompanying technological advances.[328] Since the mid-1990s, the PLAN has shifted from a small, technologically backward navy focused on coastal defense to the largest navy (numerically) in the world, capable of deploying globally and fighting high-end warfare. Given its quantitative growth and the widening scope of China's naval modernization programs, Western strategists have increasingly focused on understanding how China plans to use its naval forces in relation to its overarching grand strategy. The PLAN is important, especially in the Indo-Pacific, because "Almost all of China's primary sovereignty concerns lie in the maritime arena: Taiwan; territorial and seabed resource disputes with Japan in the East China Sea; similar disputes with Vietnam, the Philippines, Brunei, Indonesia, and Malaysia in the South China Sea; and SLOCs [sea lines of communication] across the Indian Ocean endangered by piracy in the Gulf of Aden."[329] The PLAN would play an essential role in sustaining shipping routes, augmenting overland transit created by the BRI in the face of any American blockade.

The PLAN's strategic contours have incrementally shifted over time – from near-coastal defense to active near-seas defense, and then from near-seas defense to far-seas operations beginning in the mid-2000s.[330] Growth in capability has come with these shifts.

> Indeed, for the past three decades, China has invested in combat systems— sensors, weapons, and battle management—optimized for an anti-access campaign against America's forward-based forces projecting power in the region. Such systems include satellites for covering maritime areas, back-scatter radars, intermediate-range ballistic missiles (IRBMs) with anti-ship

[327] Zhengyu Wu, "Towards Naval Normalcy: 'Open Seas Protection' and Sino–US Maritime Relations," *The Pacific Review* 32, no. 4 (2019): p. 667.

[328] Toshi Yoshihara and James R. Holmes, *Red Star Over the Pacific: China's Rise and the Challenge to U.S. Maritime Strategy* (Annapolis, MD: Naval Institute Press, revised edition, 2018).

[329] Bernard D. Cole, "The History of the Twenty-first Century Chinese Navy," *Naval War College Review* 67, no. 3 (Summer, 2014): p. 58.

[330] Nan Li, "The Evolution of China's Naval Strategy and Capabilities: From 'Near Coast' to 'Near Seas' to 'Far Seas' " in *The Chinese Navy: Expanding Capabilities, Evolving Roles*, eds. Philip Saunders, Christopher Yung, Michael Swaine and Andrew Nien-Dzu Yang (Washington, DC: National Defense University Press, 2011), pp. 109–140.

targeting capabilities, long-range cruise missiles, land-based maritime-capable bombers and attack aircraft, attack submarines, and advanced naval mines.[331]

Initially the PLAN's modernization was intended to keep any potential adversaries, including the United States, from attacking the Chinese mainland or intervening in a conflict off China's coast.[332] But the steady growth in range and offensive weaponry has caught the attention of American and regional leaders because it potentially threatens the United States, its allies and at-risk Asian sea lanes.

With time, the emergence of a capable People's Republic of China (PRC) navy has made it possible to conduct far-seas operations that could potentially challenge American naval supremacy beyond the Asian littoral. Chinese naval theorists even recommended developing overseas bases, logistic networks and doctrinal ideas such as "small battle groups" that would energize the ambition of far-seas operations.[333] Retired Rear-Admiral Michael McDevitt concluded, "[t]here is no credible information to suggest that the growing importance of 'far seas' operations is the first step in constructing a navy that that could slug it out with the U.S. Navy in a battle for sea control," but shortly thereafter he warned that the "capabilities that China is fielding in no way foreclose that option, and could be the first steps toward such a capability."[334]

An official shift away from the rhetoric of a "peaceful rise" reinforces the notion that China wants to develop military capabilities commensurate with a new grand strategy. China's defense white paper released in May 2015 provides an example as it "elevated the maritime domain within the People Liberation Army's formal strategic guidance and shifted the focus of its modernization from 'winning local wars under conditions of informationization' to "winning informationized local wars, highlighting maritime military struggle."[335]

The question now is what the PRC will do with its growing navy, potential ability to project power with aircraft carriers and amphibious ships, and newly acquired maritime facilities, ranging outward to an "emerging

[331] Sam J. Tangredi, "Anti-Access Strategies in the Pacific: The United States and China," *Parameters* 49, no. 1–2 (Spring/Summer, 2019), p. 5.

[332] "What Is A2/AD and Why Does It Matter to the United States?," Charles Koch Institute, www .charleskochinstitute.org/blog/what-is-a2ad-and-why-does-it-matter-to-the-united-states/.

[333] Li, "The Evolution of China's Naval Strategy," pp. 129–130.

[334] Michael McDevitt, "China As a Maritime Power" in *Maritime Power Building: New "Mantra" for China's Rise*, eds. Kamlesh K. Agnitori and Gurpreet S. Khourana (New Delhi: National Maritime Foundation, 2015), p. 20.

[335] Ronald O'Rourke, *China Naval Modernization: Implications for U.S. Navy Capabilities – Background and Issues for Congress*, RL33153 (Washington, DC: Congressional Research Service, 2018), p. 7.

support network"[336] for its newly-established naval base in Djibouti.[337] Both the US and India, who along with Japan maintain large and capable navies in the Indo-Pacific, have suspiciously watched both the BRI and the growth of a Chinese blue water navy capable of supporting its global commercial interests.

5.2 India and the Indo-Pacific

India's entrance into geopolitics in the Indo-Pacific has been intentionally belated. From independence in 1947 onward, its strategic approach was often depicted as neutrality on the basis of nonalignment. In practice, this meant standing aloof from superpower competition, first between the United States and the Soviet Union, and later in the rivalry between the Soviet Union and China. Independent India's first prime minister, Nehru, believed that nonalignment was consistent with its anti-imperialist, decolonization legacy. Pragmatically, it kept defense spending low and allowed the nation to focus on economic development while maintaining India's hard-won independence.[338] Until recently, India avoided taking sides while accepting help (arms sales and diplomatic support, for example), with limits and conditions, from great powers contesting the Indo-Pacific.

Nonalignment was a principle that Indian politicians often evoked but, when necessary or convenient, it was just as often transgressed. For the most part, India's two immediate post-9/11 prime ministers – Atal Bihari Vajpayee (1998–2004) and Manmohan Singh (2004–14) – remained preoccupied with domestic issues: internal development, the Naxalite rebellion and domestic terrorism.[339] The exception was the perennial issue – relations with Pakistan. As Ganguly observed, "This is because much of the energy and attention of key policymakers is sapped by the continuing confrontation with Pakistan."[340] Dual testing of nuclear weapons only served to heightened tensions.[341]

---

[336] Daniel J. Kostecka, "Places and Bases: The Chinese Navy's Emerging Support Network in the Indian Ocean," *Naval War College Review* 64, no. 1 (Winter, 2011), pp. 59–78.

[337] Jane Perlez and Chris Buckley, "China Retools Its Military with a First Overseas Outpost in Djibouti," *New York Times*, November 27, 2015, www.nytimes.com/2015/11/27/world/asia/china-military-presence-djibouti-africa.html?_r=0.

[338] Sumit Ganguly and Manjeet S. Pardesi, "Explaining Sixty Years of Indian Foreign Policy," *India Review* 4, no. 1 (2009): pp. 5–6.

[339] Rohan Mukherhee and David M. Malone, "Indian Foreign Policy and Contemporary Security Challenges," *International Affairs* 87, no. 1 (2011): pp. 87–104.

[340] Sumit Ganguly, "India's Foreign Policy Grows Up," *World Policy Journal* 20, no. 4 (Winter, 2003/2004): p. 44.

[341] S. Paul Kapur, "Ten Years of Instability in a Nuclear South Asia," *International Security* 33, no. 2 (Fall, 2008): pp. 71–94.

To some observers, Prime Minister Modi's election in 2014 marked a break with India's traditional foreign and security policies. Yet other longtime observers demurred, arguing that there has been relatively little strategic change in India's foreign policy.[342] Christine Fair notes some adjustments, from a stronger line toward Pakistan to India being "more aggressive in pursuing defense ties with other countries and appear[ing] more interested in effectuating controversial policies such as India's Cold Start Doctrine and a more confrontational posture with respect to China."[343]

Yet, as Chatterjee Miller notes, Modi is the first Indian Prime Minister since Nehru to have strong ideological underpinnings to his political program: His approach is "Nehruvianism and Hindutva overlap – in the idea of India as a leader and world teacher of superior culture, for example, or the distrust of superpower (U.S.) influence and politics."[344] Modi's Hindutva element includes the pursuit of "true national security and global recognition of India's prominent place in the world."[345]

In this reading, India's grand strategy entails the long-term objective of competing with China and the United States, both materially and as an alternative vision of economic relations and security in the Indo-Pacific region. This will require Modi to overcome the constraints of what some scholars have called "procedural pragmatism," defined as "improvising with influential and institutionalized ideas" rather than moving beyond them.[346] Two developments are emblematic of India's evolving grand strategy: the transition from the "Look East" policy of the early 1990s to the "Act East" policy of Narenda Modi; and India's determination to develop a major role in the India Ocean using its navy. Both are currently aspirational and contested, but demonstrate India's willingness to shape its external environment in the service of its domestic political and economic objectives.

---

[342] Ian Hall, "Narendra Modi and India's Normative Power," *International Affairs* 93, no. 1 (2017): pp. 113–131 (117).

[343] C. Christine Fair, "India," in Balzacq, Dombrowski and Reich, *Comparative Grand Strategy,* p. 187. See also Ankit Panda, "A Slip of the Tongue on India's Once-Hyped 'Cold Start' Doctrine?," *The Diplomat,* January 7, 2017, https://thediplomat.com/2017/01/a-slip-of-the-tongue-on-indias-once-hyped-cold-start-doctrine; Walter C. Ladwig III, "Indian Military Modernization and Conventional Deterrence in South Asia," *Journal of Strategic Studies* 38, no. 5 (2015): pp. 729–772.

[344] Manjari Chatterjee Miller, "Do Leader Ideologies Influence Foreign Policy? Nehruvianism vs. Moditva" [Book Review Roundtable on Ian Hall's *Modi and the Reinvention of Indian Foreign Policy*] *Asia Policy* 15, no. 2 (2020): p. 178, www.nbr.org/wp-content/uploads/pdfs/publications/ap15-2_modi_brrt_apr2020.pdf.

[345] Rajesh Basrur, "Modi's Foreign Policy Fundamentals: A Trajectory Unchanged," *International Affairs* 93, no. 1 (2017): pp. 7–26 (8).

[346] Manjiari Chatterjee Miller and Kate Sullivan De Estrada, "Pragmatism in Indian Foreign Policy: How Ideas Vonstrain Modi," *International Affairs* 93, no. 1 (2017): pp 27–49(29).

5.2.1 Look East, Act East

India's "Look East" policy[347]originated in the early 1990s as an effort to "forge closer and deeper economic integration with its eastern neighbours," especially through the Association of Southeast Asian Nations (ASEAN).[348] The Look East policy incrementally expanded in phases beyond this initial objective, to include a wider set of political and security issues and a large number of "target" countries to the East – "Japan, South Korea and Australia."[349] Yet despite this rhetorical focus, one assessment noted that "India has expended much talk but little action, and in its relations with its ASEAN partners, India has failed to play a major role."[350]

Prime Minister Modi added impetus to this long-standing but ineffectual policy, first by modifying the policy's name to "Act East," and then by quickening the pace of engagement. Perhaps the crown jewel in Modi's revitalization has been closer bilateral relations with Japan. Modi and Japanese former Prime Minister Shinzo Abe, by some accounts, recognized common interests in the face of growing Chinese regional ambitions and aggression.[351] Despite this positivity, limits to the Act East policy remain. This notably includes India's refusal to sign the Regional Comprehensive Economic Partnership (RCEP) agreement, a proposed free trade agreement between ASEAN and its free trade partners – Australia, Japan, India, China, South Korea and New Zealand.[352] In addition to ASEAN, "[t]o counter China's growing influence, India is networking with other like-minded countries to promote a 'free and open Indo-Pacific' through groupings such as the Asia–Africa Growth Corridor, the Quad, Malabar exercises . . ."[353]

India has therefore gradually, haltingly, asserted itself in its immediate neighborhood and beyond, especially to key economic partners (real or potential) and maritime trade routes. While the United States has encouraged the economic dimension of a strategic partnership with India, progress slowed

---

[347] Manjeet S. Pardesi, "Modi, from 'Look East' to 'Act East': Semantic or Substantive Change?" *International Studies Perspectives* 20 (2019): pp. 29–33.

[348] Thongkholal Haokip, "India's Look East Policy: Prospects and Challenges for Northeast India," *Studies in Indian Politics* 3, no. 2 (2015): pp. 198–211 (199).

[349] Lavina Lee, "India as a Nation of Consequence in Asia: The Potential and Limitations of India's 'Act East' policy," *The Journal of East Asian Affairs* 29, no. 2 (Fall/Winter, 2015): pp. 67–104 (68).

[350] Rong Ying, "The Modi Doctrine and the Future of China-India Relations," *China Institute of International Studies* 68 (2018): pp. 26–43.

[351] Rory Medcalf, *Indo-Pacific Empire: China, America and the Contest for the World's Pivotal Region* (Manchester, UK: Manchester University Press, 2020), pp. 1–3.

[352] Prabhash K. Dutta, "5 Reasons Why PM Modi Pulled out of RCEP in Bangkok," *India Today*, November 5, 2019, www.indiatoday.in/news-analysis/story/5-reasons-why-pm-modi-pulled-out-rcep-in-bangkok-1615825-2019-11-05.

[353] Lai-Ha Chan, "Can China Remake Regional Order? Contestation with India over the Belt and Road Initiative," *Global Change, Peace and Security* 32, no. 20 (2020): pp. 1–19 (1).

under the Trump administration because of American dissatisfaction with bilateral trade deficits and claims of Indian unfair trade practices.[354] This pragmatic strategy balances the needs of India's progress toward greater economic development with a recognition of the security challenges posed by China's increasingly aggressive grand strategy and its use of the PLAN as its primary instrument. Watching the PLAN's progress closely, the Indian Navy has responded with its own version of Look East, Act East.[355]

5.2.2 India's Ocean

According to Raj Narain Misra, "very few nations in the world geographically dominate an ocean area as India dominates the Indian Ocean."[356] New Delhi has always viewed the Indian Ocean as "a 'zone of peace,' free from intrusion by outside powers, reflect[ing] its concern over threats coming from the sea."[357] With limited resources, however, this meant that India had to diplomatically support its claims to the Indian Ocean's natural resources and solidify relations with other littoral states; monitor extra-regional powers (primarily the Soviet Union and the United States); and prepare to seal off Eastern chokepoints in the event of war with China. Most obviously contrary to the "zone of peace" rhetoric, the Indian Navy prepared for a "combined arms" approach to possible conflict with Pakistan.[358]

The Indian Navy's leadership has long advocated that it should take a broader role. In keeping with tradition, the 2004 "Indian Maritime Doctrine" focused "on the maritime strategy largely as a function of economic development and prosperity."[359] But, as David Brewster observed, "The 'String of Pearls' narrative has now become a prominent factor in Indian public debate about China's intentions in the Indian Ocean."[360] Although the Navy remains a secondary actor to the Army in the Indian military services, China's naval operations have justified the service's claims that it should play

---

[354] Shayerah Ilias Akhtar and K. Alan Kronstadt, "U.S.–India Trade Relations" (Congressional Research Service In Focus report, February 14, 2020).

[355] Abhijit Singh, "The Nautical Dimension of India's 'Act East' Policy," (Policy Report, S. Rajaratnam School of International Studies, Nanyang Technological University, Singapore, April 2018).

[356] Raj Narain Misra, *Indian Ocean and India's Security* (Delhi: Mittal Publications, 1986), p. 19.

[357] Gary L. Sojka, "The Missions of the Indian Navy," *Naval War College Review* 36, no. 1 (January–February, 1983): p. 4.

[358] Ashley J. Tellis, "Securing the Barrack: The Logic, Structure and Objectives of India's Naval Expansion," *Naval War College Review* 43, no. 4 (Autumn, 1990), p. 49.

[359] James R. Holmes and Toshi Yoshihara, "China's Naval Ambitions in the Indian Ocean," *Journal of Strategic Studies* 31, no. 3, (2008): pp. 367–394 (383).

[360] David Brewster, "Beyond the 'String of Pearls': Is There Really a Sino–Indian Security Dilemma in the Indian Ocean?" *Journal of the Indian Ocean Region* 10, no. 2, (2014): pp. 133–149 (139).

a larger role in the Indian Ocean. But it faces many challenges – from procurement problems and an unreliable navy industrial base, to historic distrust within the political system and government bureaucracy – in achieving its ambitions.[361] Yet Walter Ladwig's judgment is that while the Indian Navy has not substantially increased the number of its ships and other warfighting platforms, it has improved qualitatively.[362] The Malabar exercise series with other major partners – including Australia, Japan and the United States – has led to improvements in readiness and preparedness.[363]

5.3 The United States and the Indo-Pacific

National security experts were puzzled about the future of American grand strategy when Donald Trump took office. After almost three years, the direction of Trump's grand strategy was clarified by two documents. The 2017 *National Security Strategy* and the 2018 *National Defense Strategy* codified what had become apparent in Barack Obama's second term: geopolitics was entering a new era of great power conflict. The post–Cold War era of aspirational American primacy, unilateralism and indiscriminate engagement is, at least in theory, over. Russia, and especially China, pose serious threats to the United States and the geographic locus of that competition is in the Indo-Pacific.

5.3.1 Continuity and Change in the Trump Administration's Indo-Pacific Strategy

At the 2018 Shangri-La Dialogue in Singapore, then Secretary of Defense James Mattis announced the Trump administration's Indo-Pacific Strategy. He framed the strategy in broad terms: "a whole-of-government Indo-Pacific strategy which espouses the shared principles that underpin a free-and-open Indo-Pacific."[364] This framing belied a hard truth – that the bulk of the Trump administration's strategy relied on the hard power of the United States Navy (USN). Just days before, Mattis had announced that the vast combatant Pacific Command (PACOM) would be reformed into the Indo-Pacific Command

---

[361] James R. Holmes, Andrew C. Winner and Toshi Yoshihara, *Indian Naval Strategy in the Twenty-first Century* (New York: Routledge, 2009), pp. 79– 95.

[362] Walter C. Ladwig III, "Drivers of Indian Naval Expansion" in *The Rise of the Indian Navy: Internal Vulnerabilities, External Challenges*, ed. Harsh Pant (New York: Routledge, 2014), pp. 19–40.

[363] Piyush Ghasiya, "Changing Geopolitical Dynamics and Malabar Exercise," *Centre for Air Power Studies* 68 (August 16, 2017): p. 1.

[364] Secretary of Defense James N. Mattis and John Chipman, Director-General and Chief Executive, International Institute for Strategic Studies, "Remarks by Secretary Mattis at Plenary Session of the 2018 Shangri-La Dialogue," June 2, 2018, www.defense.gov/ Newsroom/Transcripts/Transcript/Article/1538599/remarks-by-secretary-mattis-at-plenary-session-of-the-2018-shangri-la-dialogue/.

(INDOPACOM).[365] Although Mattis downplayed China's significance in this decision, outgoing PACOM Command Admiral "Harry" Harris was blunt: "Great power competition is back ... I believe we are reaching an inflection point in history ... [a] geo-political competition between free and oppressive visions is taking place in the Indo-Pacific."[366] The United States would provide the main military guarantees against great power aggression (effectively China) and support the nation's regional allies and partners.

There was a tension between Mattis's broad vision, the geo-economic realities of the Indo-Pacific region, the Trump administration's reliance on military instruments and the United States overextended military capabilities. Candidate Trump had criticized the Obama administration's "Asia Rebalance." He pledged to abandon the Trans-Pacific Partnership (TPPA), impose high tariffs on Chinese imports and declare the PRC a "currency manipulator."[367] Yet while Trump did forsake the TPPA, as well as imposing tariffs on China and damaging bilateral relations with key regional partners, the military Rebalance continued. In response to China's growing capacity and assertiveness, the USN is shifting toward a 60/40 split of its forces between the Indo-Pacific and the rest of the world.

5.3.2 The Naval Dimensions

The US Pacific Fleet "consists of approximately 200 ships/submarines, nearly 1,200 aircraft, and more than 130,000 Sailors and civilians."[368] Numbers (of warships, warplanes, soldiers and sailors) matter, of course, but China's military, especially the PLAN, can match American forward deployments in many respects. How does the United States plan to use its capabilities? The short answer is in a traditional way: The USN, like all American military forces, is committed to maintaining access to the global commons in Asia as elsewhere for itself, and its allies and partners. The issue is whether the USN has sufficient resources – ships, air wings and manpower – to fulfill the promise of the Asia

---

[365] A geographic combatant command is in charge "of using and integrating United States Army, Navy, Air Force and Marine Corps forces within the USINDOPACOM area of responsibility (AOR) to achieve U.S. national security objectives while protecting national interests"; www .pacom.mil/About-USINDOPACOM/USPACOM-Area-of-Responsibility/.

[366] Tara Copp, "INDOPACOM, It Is: US Pacific Command gets renamed," *Military Times*, May 30, 2018, www.militarytimes.com/news/your-military/2018/05/30/indo-pacom-it-is-pacific-command-gets-renamed/.

[367] Stewart M. Patrick, "Trump and World Order: The Return of Self-Help," *Foreign Affairs* 96, no. 2 (March/April, 2017), p. 55.

[368] "U.S. Pacific Fleet Advances Indo-Pacific Regional Maritime Security and Enhances Stability," www.cpf.navy.mil/about/.

Rebalance, especially if the mission is to project power in the western Pacific against the increasingly capable PLAN.

Candidate Trump promised that he would expand the USN to 355 ships, representing an increase of more than 50 vessels from its peak during the Bush and Obama administrations. As president, he signed the 2017 National Defense Act making this goal official policy.[369] Yet it foundered on budgetary realities.[370] And Biden's election consolidates the view that it is unlikely that the USN will receive a budgetary boost to sustain current operating tempos indefinitely, much less achieve the numbers required to deter or win a naval war with China. A gap exists between the rhetoric surrounding current United States grand strategy and its implementation in the Indo-Pacific that is unlikely to be reduced during Biden's presidency.

American strategists endorse the view that the reorientation of American national security should face toward the Indo-Pacific. But the strategic implications of insufficient budgets and political realities are unclear. One possibility is a movement from unilateralism toward multilateral engagement to compensate for the theater's vast geography and reduced American capacity – a greater reliance on American regional partners and allies. The likely result is even more pressure on burden sharing (especially with India). The 2019 Indo-Pacific Strategy presages this development: "The department [Department of Defense] is reinforcing its commitment to established alliances and partnerships, while also expanding and deepening relationships with new partners who share our respect for sovereignty, fair and reciprocal trade, and the rule of law."[371] But there is no doubt that, whatever the outcome, the US is having to adapt as its primacy in the Indo-Pacific has dwindled.

The traditional American primacy strategy is therefore now in conflict with the new geography. The United States is trying to hold on to the vestiges of American dominance as China and India gain confidence and maritime capacity, but is having to adapt. In the next decade, the enlarged Indo-Pacific as a theater of operations presents an irresolvable tension that will likely entail a shift to a new strategy that already appears, at least embryonically, under way.

---

[369] David B. Larter, "Trump Just Made a 355-ship Navy National Policy," *Defense News*, December 13, 2017, www.defensenews.com/congress/2017/12/14/trump-just-made-355-ships -national-policy/.

[370] David Axe, "The U.S. Navy Is Struggling to Grow," *The National Interest*, July 18, 2018, https://nationalinterest.org/blog/buzz/us-navy-struggling-grow-26071.

[371] Department of Defense, *Indo-Pacific Strategy Report*, June 1, 2019, https://media.defense.gov/ 2019/Jul/01/2002152311/-1/-1/1/DEPARTMENT-OF-DEFENSE-INDO-PACIFIC-STRATEGY- REPORT-2019.PDF.

5.4 Conclusion

The Indo-Pacific region is a relatively new strategic framing with deep regional roots. Today, "The raison d'etre of the Indo-Pacific is maritime security: developing institutions and governance arrangement to manage the SLOC interdependencies linking countries on the Pacific and Indian Ocean rims."[372] As China has risen, it has developed a more assertive grand strategy based on both trans-regional economic integration following both sea- and land-based transportation routes and a more powerful military. Its emergence not only threatens its immediate neighbors but has captured the attention of Indian and American strategists and policymakers.[373]

India has expanded its strategic ambitions as a result of China's challenge and its own internal political and economic development. It has sought to influence Indo-Pacific states beyond its immediate neighborhood through Modi's "Act East" policy. This more expansive regional political vision has been accompanied by a more capable navy, with a presence not only in the Indian Ocean but, at least aspirationally, further East. It has developed stronger relations with Japan and, stutteringly, "India has significantly expanded the scale and scope of its bilateral engagement with the United States."[374] Despite its lesser capabilities, India seeks to behave more like a great power by balancing China and perhaps even joining a democratic coalition to contain its neighbor.

For almost a decade after 9/11, the United States was distracted by its interventions in the greater Middle East and the Global War on Terror. As the wars in Afghanistan and Iraq waned, it was no longer feasible to minimize the impact of China on American interests globally, much less the western Pacific, where the United States has played a leading role for over a century. Rebalancing, an adaptive strategy, reversed both a period of relative neglect and decisively shifted the Transatlantic versus Asia focus in American foreign, economic and security policies. President Trump, after a slow start caused in part by dismantling the trans-Pacific economic regionalism initiated by President Obama, accelerated this process by refocusing on the direct economic threat posed by China. As Lindsey Ford noted in spring 2020, "obvious incongruities between the president's instincts – as encapsulated by his 'America

---

[372] Jeffrey D. Wilson, "Rescaling to the Indo-Pacific: From Economic to Security-Driven Regionalism in Asia," *East Asia* 35 (2018): pp. 177–196 (181).

[373] See essays on India's responses to China's rise in Harsh V. Pant, ed., *China Ascendant: Its Rise and Implications* (New Delhi: Harper Collins, 2019).

[374] Harsh V. Pant and Yogeshi Joshi, "Indo–US Relations under Modi: The Strategic Logic Underlying the Embrace," *International Affairs* 93, no. 1 (2017): pp. 133–146 (146).

First' slogan – and the ambitions of the administration's Indo-Pacific strategy have undermined its implementation."[375]

Although great power war in the Indo-Pacific is not inevitable, the grand strategies of its three largest nations appear incompatible. India and the United State have taken major steps to resist China's assertiveness from the South China Sea to the east coast of Africa to the Eurasian hinterlands. In grand strategic terms, the United States seems bent on maintaining its military primacy, fortified before Trump by multilateral diplomacy and institution building. Trump's promise of a 355-ship USN appeared to commit the nation to maritime dominance, while his budgetary and diplomatic failures undermined the underpinnings of US grand strategy in the region.

China, of course, remains the wild card. If it maintains the assertiveness of the Xi era and enjoys sufficient economic growth to maintain its regional material advantages –ranging from the PLAN to foreign direct investment and aid – it will be difficult for either India or the United States to moderate, much less contain, their rival. This instability might threaten the smaller states of the region, leading to capitulation to Chinese preferences and demands.

6. A Brief Conclusion

The field of grand strategy lacks the standards and methods associated with a progressive research program.[376] This Element has attempted to contribute to its development. Our primary goal has been to introduce the notion of comparison to the study of grand strategy: between types, over time and across space. As in many other fields of political science, America has long been treated as sui generis and thus incomparable in the study of grand strategy.[377] That view is predicated on the belief that it is the biggest, most important state to which others must geostrategically respond. The American notion of its own "exceptionalism" often supports this claim.[378] The only other contemporary states whose grand strategies are worth evaluating are reputedly China and Russia,

---

[375] Lindsey Ford, "The Trump Administration and the 'Free and Open Indo-Pacific', " Brookings Institution, May, 2020, www.brookings.edu/wp-content/uploads/2020/05/fp_20200505_free_o pen_indo_pacific.pdf.

[376] Balzacq, Dombrowski and Reich, "Is Grand Strategy a Research Program?"

[377] This is a voluminous literature, both old and new. For some variants, see James W. Ceaser, "The Origins and Character of American Exceptionalism," *American Political Thought* 1, no. 1 (Spring, 2012), pp. 3–28; Louis Hartz, *The Liberal Tradition in America* (New York: Harcourt, Brace and World, 1955); Seymour Martin Lipset, *American Exceptionalism: A Double-edged Sword* (New York: Norton, 1997); Charles A. Murray, *American Exceptionalism: An Experiment in History* (Washington, DC: AEI Press, 2013).

[378] Geoffrey Hodgson, *The Myth of American Exceptionalism* (New Haven, CT: Yale University Press, 2010).

two shaping great powers. But their ends, ways and means are supposedly so different that even they are not usefully compared to the United States.

We believe that exceptionalist perspective has problems. First, geostrategically, it ignores the complex dynamics of a global system which may be rapidly mutating, hastened by the consequences of the COVID-19 pandemic. The ways that states can wield influence across different domains, such as cyberspace, is growing. This capacity extends beyond the militarized domains often associated with US grand strategy to diplomatic and economic ones, and brings into focus a world well beyond China and Russia. India, as we have demonstrated, is playing an increasingly important role, economically and militarily. Brazil, with its control over the Amazon, is crucial in battling climate change. Even smaller powers such as Israel, Pakistan or Saudi Arabia can destabilize the global system, whether through the sales of advanced military technologies or oil, through Jihadism or as a result of war.

Critics may argue that there may be limited utility in comparing the ways or means of the United States relative to many of these states. Yet contrasts, as much as similarities, may provide useful lessons for policymakers. There is much to learn about how others formulate and implement grand strategies in a world where, for example, North Korea (stubbornly) or Iran (more agilely) have repeatedly been able to outmaneuver successive US presidents on the issue of their nuclear programs. In the absence of an interactive approach, American grand strategy, despite the United States' enormous intellectual and institutional capacity, risks being more reactive than proactive.

Second, conceptually, the notion of comparison expands the framework of analysis intellectually as well as the universe of cases worth studying. Comparative frameworks provide a building block towards causative theory building. But the field of grand strategy lacks indigenous theories. Scholars often draw on balance of power, hegemony or power transition theories to substantiate their prescriptions. New theories could explain why some grand strategies endure and others change, or why similar ones have contrasting consequences. Containment, for example, has been described as a grand strategy but it often led to contrasting American behavior when it came to issues like deterrence or compellence, democracy promotion or subversion. Comparing national strategies over time or across states may therefore encourage a better understanding of the causative, interactive dynamics of domestic and systemic factors, building a focus on the preferences of presidents or the structural determinants of the global system that now predominate.

Third, comparison helps us recognize that different states now use grand strategies for vastly different purposes. The initial definition focused on the winning of wars (Clausewitz). That evolved in some quarters into the winning of peace (Liddell Hart). A further sub-element then stressed promoting capitalism and democracy. These elements have always encountered opposition when the study of grand strategy has expanded. But in the age of COVID-19 and a climate crisis, grand strategizing can reasonably be about large or small states that adeptly strategize to fight epidemics, rising seas, growing poverty or increasing droughts. Many states now strategize to address these issues both at home and abroad. If political science is still the study of power, if these are the major threats that many states face, and if the evidence suggests that states do employ the ends, ways and means we associate with grand strategy, then it seems arbitrary (and perhaps too convenient for some scholars) to simply define them as outside the contours of legitimate study. The onus is on those who rankle at the idea to demonstrate why states should be excluded from comparison, rather than to assume that they should be.

So, what of future research? Here, we have used the United States as a familiar benchmark in offering an unfamiliar approach. We have attempted to demonstrate that systematic comparison is feasible. Section 3, on types, asked and answered a series of questions about the forms and substance of different approaches that may, if suitably amended to allow for context, extend beyond the United States to other great and regional powers. Many states predominantly sponsor UN initiatives (e.g. Norway). But others may seek regional primacy (Iran) or isolationism (North Korea). Section 4, on time, attempted to demonstrate that spotlighting key attributes can augment the work of historians, especially when systematically focusing on the relationship between key domestic and systemic factors. Finally, section 5, on the Indo-Pacific, provided an opportunity to demonstrate that grand strategies are interactive, and sometimes it is the United States that adapts.

The options for building on this analysis are too numerous to list. But candidates might begin with national studies of regional powers, extending beyond those we have discussed here to others such as Australia or Turkey. Another option is to focus on Asian or European states such as Germany, Japan, South Korea, Sweden or the United Kingdom. A third option is the study of small, rich states and city-states – stretching from the Gulf states to Singapore or Taiwan – which have obvious credentials, based as much on their history and geography as on their current geostrategic significance.

Finally, scholars assume that the United States uses a grand strategy as a blueprint to control or shape the global system – while everyone else adapts. In this, scholars have built on studies of the United Kingdom's historical roles in creating and then dominating both globalization and international security from the late eighteenth to the mid-twentieth centuries.[379] But the United Kingdom did have to adapt and, as section 5 demonstrates, the United States has to do so now in the face of China's rising economic and security challenge. A key question therefore becomes why and how do states balance controlling, shaping or adapting? This kind of question is antithetical to the current field.

Our modest effort in this Element has simply been to attempt to elucidate how the unique is really the comparable. But a research program awaits that could benefit academics and policymakers in equal measure.

---

[379] Aptly reflecting the view of many contemporary American scholars, David Gethin Morgan-Owen writes of an "Anglo-American epoch" beginning with scholars like Julian Corbett, J. F. C. Fuller and Basil Liddell Hart (and subsequently Michael Howard and Andrew Lambert) who believed that, "The British believed that grand strategy was something only they needed to do, owing to their unique position of global maritime and financial power"; David Gethin Morgan-Owen, "History and the Perils of Grand Strategy," *Journal of Modern History* 92 (June, 2020), pp. 351–385 (353).

Acknowledgments

The authors would like to thank Thierry Balzacq for his suggestions, friendship and support, and Rachael Shaffer for her invaluable research assistance. Jonathan Caverley was a patient intellectual sounding board for Peter Dombrowski throughout the project. Peter thanks Ann Martino and Johanna Dombrowski for their usual love and support. Simon Reich thanks the Gerda Henkel Foundation for its financial support and Ariane Chebel d'Appollonia for her unstinting love, support and advice.

Cambridge Elements ☰

International Relations

Series Editors

Jon C. W. Pevehouse
University of Wisconsin-Madison
Jon C. W. Pevehouse is the Vilas Distinguished Achievement Professor of Political Science at the University of Wisconsin-Madison. He has published numerous books and articles in IR in the fields of international political economy, international organizations, foreign policy analysis, and political methodology. He is a former editor of the leading IR field journal, *International Organization*.

Tanja A. Börzel
Freie Universität Berlin
Tanja A. Börzel is the Professor of political science and holds the Chair for European Integration at the Otto-Suhr-Institute for Political Science, Freie Universität Berlin. She holds a PhD from the European University Institute, Florence, Italy. She is coordinator of the Research College "The Transformative Power of Europe," as well as the FP7-Collaborative Project "Maximizing the Enlargement Capacity of the European Union" and the H2020 Collaborative Project "The EU and Eastern Partnership Countries: An Inside-Out Analysis and Strategic Assessment." She directs the Jean Monnet Center of Excellence "Europe and its Citizens."

Edward D. Mansfield
University of Pennsylvania
Edward D. Mansfield is the Hum Rosen Professor of Political Science, University of Pennsylvania. He has published well over 100 books and articles in the area of international political economy, international security, and international organizations. He is Director of the Christopher H. Browne Center for International Politics at the University of Pennsylvania and former program co-chair of the American Political Science Association.

Associate Editors

Jeffrey T. Checkel *Simon Fraser University*
Miles Kahler *American University*
Sarah Kreps *Cornell University*
Anna Leander *Graduate Institute Geneva, Institute of International Relations (PUC-Rio), and Copenhagen Business School*
Stefanie Walter *University of Zurich*

About the Series
Cambridge Elements in International Relations publishes original research on key topics in the field. The series includes manuscripts addressing international security, international political economy, international organizations, and international relations theory. Our objective is to publish cutting edge research that engages crucial topics in each of these issue areas, especially multi-method research that may yield longer studies than leading journals in the field will accommodate.

Cambridge Elements ☰

International Relations

Elements in the Series

Printed in the United States
by Baker & Taylor Publisher Services